Chevrolet History:
1955-1957

By John D. Robertson

Published by **Cars & Parts Magazine,**
The Voice of the Collector Car Hobby Since 1957

Cars & Parts Magazine is a division of Amos Press Inc.,
911 Vandemark Road, Sidney, Ohio 45365

Also publishers of:
Catalog of American Car ID Numbers 1950-59
Catalog of American Car ID Numbers 1960-69
Catalog of American Car ID Numbers 1970-79
Catalog of Camaro ID Numbers 1967-93
Catalog of Chevy Truck ID Numbers 1946-72
Catalog of Ford Truck ID Numbers 1946-72
Catalog of Chevelle, Malibu & El Camino ID Numbers 1964-87
Catalog of Pontiac GTO ID Numbers 1964-74
Catalog of Corvette ID Numbers 1953-93
Catalog of Mustang ID Numbers 19641/2-93
Catalog of Thunderbird ID Numbers 1955-93
Catalog of Firebird ID Numbers 1967-93
Catalog of Oldsmobile 4-4-2, W-Machine & Hurst/Olds ID Numbers 1964-91
Catalog of Chevy Engine V-8 Casting Numbers 1955-93
Salvage Yard Treasures of America
Ultimate Collector Car Price Guide
Ultimate Muscle Car Price Guide
Automobiles of America
The Resurrection of Vicky
Peggy Sue — 1957 Chevrolet Restoration
Suzy Q.: Restoring a '63 Corvette Sting Ray
How to Build a Dune Buggy
Corvette: American Legend (The Beginning)
Corvette: American Legend (1954-55 Production)
Corvette: American Legend (1956 Racing Success)
Corvette: American Legend (1957 Fuel Injection/283 V-8)
A Pictorial History of Chevrolet 1929-1939
A Pictorial History of Chevrolet 1940-1954

Dedication

Over the years, I've been touched by many people who have been involved in some way with my automotive obsession. Some were really nice folks who sold me a car cheap or helped me get one running or came up with hard to find parts. Then there were those who have been more involved in the events that directly led up to this series of books. When I first became involved with the archives, there were three people already on the scene who have now been pushing this snowball uphill for about eight years. Tom Freiman, Kim Schroeder and Larry Kinsel have been performing miracles like routine assignments and are totally responsible for creating the archive that other archives are now benchmarking. Without their tireless zeal for developing systems and then improving them repeatedly, the archives would probably not have gotten off the ground. These three were usually still working when I went home to play with cars. Future students of General Motors history will have a lot more to work with because of Tom, Kim and Larry.

Over 20 years ago another car guy showed up at the Sandy Corporation as the editor of several Chevrolet publications. Like myself, he liked old Chevys and we had plenty to talk about. About a year later, I left to go to another agency. Bob Stevens went on to become the editor of *Cars & Parts*. Since then, we have walked the aisles of Hershey, Carlisle, Hoosier and numerous smaller Michigan and Ohio swap meets. We've even owned three of the same cars at different times. I've written a few articles for Bob over the years so it was logical to talk with Bob when I thought about doing these books. Bob was supportive and I decided to proceed. Bob has now edited three of these books. He is a rare blend of professional and hobbyist who has brought enjoyable reading to car people for two decades.

On July 2, 1998, after 22 years of undisciplined divorced life, I married Catherine in Lee County, Florida. She has encouraged me to work on this project and tolerated the times when piles of photos, reference materials and other junk took over the kitchen table and, sometimes, most of the kitchen. She has been enthused and excited as I have bought car after car. When we hit 18 cars, she finally asked if we could afford it. Of course I lied. When car number 20 arrived I confessed that, while I'm having a lot of fun, it isn't easy trying to maintain all these cars. Catherine had an idea. When spring arrives I will be advertising six cars. Thanks Cath, I wouldn't have thought of that.

Contents

Preface

Readers who have seen previous books in this series and are familiar with the origin of the GM Media Archives are encouraged to skip ahead while I take a few moments to tell newcomers about the amazing archives. The nucleus of the GM Media Archives is the collection of the former GM Photographic, which was in the Argonaut "B" building on Milwaukee Avenue behind Detroit's General Motors building. In approximately 1954 or 1955, the collection was moved to a large dingy room in an out of the way corner of the 9th floor. Known as "the vinegar room" because of the distinctive aroma, this room was filled with floor-to-ceiling file drawers. In the late 1980s, several visionaries realized that this unique corporate treasure must be preserved and sought approval to locate and bring together all such collections within the corporation. The goal was to make historical images available to all corporate users and their agencies.

In the early 1990s the word was spread to other areas within GM that a department had been created within GM whose charter was to assure the safe retention of and future accessibility to all photographic images within the corporation. Some additional collections were transferred to the archives and others were electronically scanned while the original images remained with their originating units. The GM Media Archives is truly global in scope with all GM worldwide products represented and more fascinating images arriving weekly.

A dedicated group of skilled researchers and professional preservationists works with the most technologically advanced storage and retrieval equipment available. All automotive images are reviewed for historic significance. Those deemed relevant are identified by make, model and year, with any pertinent information tagged, and are then indexed for fast, accurate retrieval. Processed images are sleeved and filed in fresh envelopes before being stored in a new, more environmentally friendly facility for permanent storage. The oldest images in the collection are now more than 100 years old, the newest portray proposals for the next decade.

For obvious reasons, including space, travel expenses and security, it will not be possible to parade the world's Chevrolet fans through the archives. This series of books is the next best thing, however, and I hope you will capture, while reading it, some of the pleasure I've derived from compiling it.

John D. Robertson

About the Author

While the author admires all three years of the midfifties Chevys, his favorite is the 1956, as seen here in a Sport Coupe two-door hardtop painted a rare springtime color, Inca Silver, with India Ivory two-toning.

John Robertson fondly remembers the world as it was when the Chevrolets covered in this book were new cars. Imagine, if you will, being a senior at Redford High in car-crazy Detroit in the fall of 1954, when the 1955 model cars, most either all new or drastically facelifted, were introduced. John was one of those long-ago kids who debated the as-yet-untested merits of those cars. His father being a Chrysler employee, John's inclinations were to argue loudly, if not skillfully, the virtues of the 1955 Plymouth. No apologizing for an ugly Plymouth this time, and a brand new O.H.V. V-8 to blow those Fords in the weeds! Wrong! It soon became evident that the only Fords those Plymouths were going to beat would be 1954 models and that the 1955 Chevrolet with its high-revving V-8 would annihilate both of them.

John recalls that the Ford and Plymouth fans, realizing that this was not a year to discuss performance, seized on Chevrolet's unorthodox Ferrari-inspired front styling and professed to know for sure that Chevrolet would be making a mid-year change. Ferrari grille not withstanding, most of his classmates who could afford such things bought a new Chevy, including one whose six with overdrive clobbered John's faster-than-average 1950 Dodge — big time, every time. Off the line, rolling start, top end, everything. The ones who bought V-8s (that would be most of them) wound up racing each other because everybody else was hiding.

On the first day of John's summer job at the Chrysler Proving Grounds at Chelsea in 1955, he was assigned to guard a truck crossing on the banked high-speed track. After a few boring hours watching the occasional car run past, he heard a roar in the distance and saw, not one, but two, sets of headlights down the track. Soon a '55 Bel Air passed, followed at an ever-increasing distance, by a '55 Plymouth Belvedere.

About 15 minutes later John again heard a roar and again saw two sets of headlights. This time, the Chevrolet was in the process of whipping a '55 Chrysler Windsor Deluxe. A little more time passed and the familiar roar was heard, two more sets of headlights and a '55 Chrysler 300 blew past with the Bel Air bringing up the rear. Not exactly a fair match but, what the heck, Chrysler was paying the bill. He also noted that several of the guys at the Chrysler grounds had bought new Chevys. Interesting. In the fall, John transferred to an apprenticeship as a clay modeler at Chrysler styling. He bought an early Hemi Chrysler, which made great impressive noises while being soundly beaten by Chevrolets.

At 19, and unable to get financing for a new car, John tried another approach, building up a hot '52 Ford Flathead which was dropped in a '51 club coupe. John learned how to change transmissions, lots of transmissions on that sorry Ford, but he didn't beat any Chevy V-8s. Then came college followed by marriage, children and a series of cheap old cars. After a period of teaching school John opened a used car lot and, on that lot, got his first Chevy V-8. This would be the first of many 55-56-57 Chevrolets, sedans, sport coupes, convertibles, and even a Nomad he would own.

Of all those Chevys, his favorite was a '56 Bel Air Sport coupe with power pack and overdrive. Ever the rebel, he still prefers the '56 Chevy over the '55 and '57 models. The used car lot being less than a

smashing success, John rejoined Chrysler and spent a few years in the leasing department. In 1969, John joined the Jam Handy Organization in an engineering liaison capacity on the Chevrolet account. Ten years later John jumped to Ross Roy Advertising on the Chrysler account. By 1983 John was back serving Chevrolet at Campbell-Ewald Advertising. Two years later, John moved across the street to General Motors Photographic as a product information specialist until joining the newly formed GM Media Archives where he is still employed identifying automotive images.

Through the years John's life-long interest in antique cars has matured into a full-blown obsession. Even during times of personal economic disaster he managed to hang on to some sort of collector car. Sometimes, when the obsession is especially prevalent, an eclectic bunch of old cars can be found filling the garages, clogging the driveways, spilling across the lawn, and finally resting in rented garages all around metropolitan Detroit. As this was written, there were 20 vehicles, titled and licensed in John's name. Recent additions were three old limos from the '40s and '50s.

John and his recent bride, Catherine, live in Shelby Township, Mich., about 30 miles north of Detroit. By a happy turn of fate, Catherine is also into cars with a '77 Corvette, a '78 Seville, and a Chevy-powered '37 Chrysler coupe in her part of the garage. Their favorites are the Vette, a '70 Impala convertible, a maroon '49 Fleetline Deluxe two-door loaded with authorized factory accessories, and a Sierra Gold and Adobe Beige '57 Bel Air Sport Sedan four-door hardtop with the 283 V-8 and Powerglide.

Introduction

While this book concerns itself with the 1955, 1956, and 1957 Chevrolets, it is useful to understand the events in the American auto industry that influenced the evolutionary development of those remarkable vehicles that were so right for their time and the decades that have followed.

In the very early years of the auto industry, survival was often based on the product's ability to operate on a more or less regular basis. As the vehicles got better, buyer expectations rose and they began to figure that dependability should be taken for granted. The best selling cars, the Curved Dash Olds, the Buick Model 10 and Ford's Model T had been affordable to almost every new car buyer. As production climbed, Ford continually lowered the price of the Model T, attracting even more buyers. With the arrival of Chevrolet and other competitors "greater value" joined "low price" as a purchase motivator. Due to Ford's incredible volume, it was impossible for other manufacturers to compete with Ford on a price basis. Alfred Sloan of General Motors realized that it would be possible, and profitable, to add some features that buyers desired and sell a Chevrolet for more money because it was more car. The trick was to stay in more or less the same price range. The consumers compared the products and, in increasing numbers throughout the 1920s, agreed that the Chevrolet was worth the extra money. It was O.K. to pay a little more if you got added value in the product. Things like advanced mechanical, comfort, or convenience features, for example. This is the issue that gradually brought the Model T down throughout the 1920s resulting in sales leadership for Chevrolet. The third issue, performance, was raised in 1929 when Chevrolet introduced a reliable six-cylinder engine to compete with Ford. While not the first with a low cost six, Chevrolet was the first with a durable low cost six. It was this product action that prompted Henry Ford to develop his Flathead V-8 for 1932. Of course, Chevrolet's move to six cylinders was largely motivated by the smoothness of operation that characterized a six when compared to the four cylinder cars of the time. Within a couple of years, Willys would be the only major manufacturer of four cylinder passenger cars. Through the thirties and up to the immediate post war period of the forties, all manufacturers continued to refine their engines for greater power as weight increases absorbed portions of that increased power. During this period, Ford built up a loyal following among the younger crowd to whom the Ford V-8 was the performance car. Chevrolet continued to build a huge owner base on the concept of

added value, while both led the market with their low price appeal. The third player in that game was Plymouth, which also operated on the concept of a little more car for a little more money.

In 1949, Cadillac and Oldsmobile launched new high-compression overhead valve V-8s. The Oldsmobile engine, dramatically named "Rocket," was available in a new, moderately priced series called the 88. It was somewhat a stretch, but the 88 was within the reach of at least some Ford and Chevrolet buyers. Overnight, the Olds, which to that point had a reputation for solid if stodgy reliability, became the icon for modern high performance. In 1950, the public and the rest of the auto industry watched Olds and Cadillac building on their performance reputation. In 1951 Chrysler and Studebaker joined the move to overhead valve V-8 power and DeSoto and Lincoln jumped on board in 1952. In 1953 Buick and Dodge adopted V-8 power. The Korean conflict, which resulted in material shortages, delayed several of these introductions by a year or two. Dodge, for example had expected to field their new car in 1952 while Mercury had expected a new OHV engine that didn't arrive until 1954. Ford got into overhead valves with the new I-Block 6 of 1952 and followed up with the new Y-Block V-8 of 1954 (1955 in Canada). There was definitely a horsepower race going on and the public loved it.

Ford was the first of the major manufacturers to get an all-new car to the market after WWII. In June of 1948, with the postwar sellers market beginning to soften a bit, Ford launched their 1949 models. They were modern in design and incorporated chassis and suspension improvements that finally separated Fords from their Model A ancestors. These Fords came very close to negating the "more car" argument that had so successfully contributed to Chevrolet's status as number one in sales. Chevrolet, of course, soon introduced the beautifully styled 1949 models which drew on their kinship to Cadillac to look very impressive. Over the next few years, Chevrolet and Ford continued to add features and models making the low-price field a very attractive place in which to shop. Of course, as more and more glitz was added, as coupes gave way to hardtops, those lower-middle price Oldsmobile 88's began to get closer in price and started to do their own conquesting in the low price field. It was a lot like the Chevy vs. Ford story of the 1920s, but this time the added value was horsepower. Cadillac, Chrysler, Lincoln, DeSoto all had big modern engines but they were handicapped by high prices. Studebaker's nice little V-8 of 1951 was not much of a threat because it was just that: little. (The author has often wondered what the future would have held if Studebaker had started out with about 260 cid in 1951.) By 1953 Chevrolet's 235 cid as used with Powerglide was a smooth, quiet, modern, durable, and pretty gutsy power plant with full-pressure lubrication and hydraulic lifters. However, the writing was on the wall: if you want sell cars you better offer them with a modern, high-compression, OHV V-8. With this scenario building in 1952, General Motors began taking the right steps to be sure that the giant Chevrolet division didn't get out of step with the market in 1955.

When Ed Cole left Cadillac's Cleveland tank plant in 1952 it was to become Chevrolet's chief engineer with broad responsibilities for the development of the 1955 product. Cole immediately set about gathering a team that would start with a clean sheet and work up an all-new Chevrolet. This wasn't going to be a case of stuffing a new engine in an existing vehicle (like Ford would be doing for 1954). Of course, it was the recognized need to be there with a new engine (and a new image) that drove the development of the entire car. Cole knew that he wanted a lot of potential packed into a relatively small, light engine. Around that would be built a car that would take advantage of that engine but not stress it. When Cole arrived at Chevrolet there was already a V-8 in development. A 231 cid V-8. Considering that the 6-cylinder it was supposed to upstage was 235-cid, that would have been a mistake along the lines of that made by Studebaker in 1951. Besides, this 231-cid engine didn't break any new ground. It was strongly influenced by the 331-cid engine that Cole had helped develop for the 1949 Cadillac. Cole discarded the proposed engine and began setting up the criteria that would result in the innovative 265 cid V-8 of 1955. The innovations were not limited to the engine itself. In fact, the engine design would not have been possible without parallel innovations in the fields of "green sand" casting and manufacturing. The most important single contributor to the legendary performance of the early small block Chevrolet was the uniquely simple valve train design which eliminated rocker shafts and replaced the traditional heavy rocker arms with light-weight, precision stamped arms, resulted in the high-revving characteristics for which it is so well known.

At announcement time, the 1955 Chevrolets were something of a shock to traditional Chevrolet buyers. These low, brightly colored cars with wraparound windshields were going to take some getting used to. For one thing, those seats were right on the floor. And that eggcrate grille angled in there between that flat hood and the flat bumper. Supposed to look like something called a Ferrari. Sounds foreign. In 1956 *Auto Age* magazine had this to say about the Chevrolet front end. "Last year (1955) Chevrolet did come out with a rather unique and foreign-looking front grille treatment but as the months went by, GM stylists became less and less convinced that this unique approach was a wise one. Accordingly they have expanded the grille to the outer extremities of the fenders in their 1956 product giving the whole front end of the car a more massive — and more normal — look." Eventually a later generation of collectors grew up loving the '55 grille. And the new V-8, as it turned out, was the hottest thing going in 1955.

The 1956 Chevrolet has not enjoyed quite the same collector car status that the 1955 and 1957 models have. The author, who has loved 1956 Chevrolets from day one, is running against the herd on this issue. Given enough storage space and an unexpected windfall, he wants to add a '55, a '56, to the '57 currently in his collection but freely admits preference for the 1956. The facelift for 1956 was a very good one, adding the appearance of length that was a positive attribute at the time. The colors, in and out, were cheerful and optimistic, completely in sync with the public outlook at the end of Ike's first term. A 1956 Chevrolet was just a happy car. It was happy to be in or to look at. While retaining the 235 cid six and the 265 cid V-8, both were improved. The author, a used car dealer in the early '60s, recalls that there were several things to be very careful of when buying 1955 Chevrolets, especially at the dealer auctions. If it was a six it could be a big-time oil burner. The problem, it was said, was in the new air cleaner for 1955 six cylinder models. It just couldn't stand up to extremely dusty conditions and, if not meticulously maintained, dirt would begin getting through the filter, wiping out the rings. When buying 1955 V-8 models you had to watch for a miss. That could indicate that there was a more serious problem inside — a broken piston. When that cylinder fired the piston could be heard so people would install a dead spark plug because a miss was easier to pass off than a clanking piston. While each of these problems could be found in 1956 models they were far more common in 1955s. The 1956 bodies were also improved. While everything rusted in the salt belt in those days, the 1955's were more likely to have patched front fender caps. The downside was the rustout that came later in the life cycle to the wrap-around grille extensions of the 1956 models. Even as a young man, the author preferred the seating position, riding qualities and sound isolation of the 1954 Chevrolet to that of the 1955, although the 1955 cornered much better than the 1954. By 1956, much of the sophistication had returned while the enhanced handling qualities were maintained. In short, the 1955 Chevrolet was a nice car and it got even better in 1956. When making a comparison between the 1956 and 1957 Chevrolets, most points, for either side, will be subjective. One that is not subjective is the availability, in 1957, of the bigger-than-life, all-time-great, 283 V-8. And, of course, in limited numbers, fuel injection. As this is being written, a 1957 fuel injection Bel Air convertible sold at auction for a record $85,000. Returning to the subjective, some folks think the 1956 is the better looking of the two. Many folks would challenge that line of thought. When pondering it, just remember which Chevrolet was outsold by Ford and why.

Luck, sheer unadulterated luck, was with Chevrolet in 1957 and is largely responsible for the lofty image that the 1957 Chevrolet enjoys. The 1957 Chevrolet is an icon, the symbol of good times in the '50s. That wasn't always the case and it doesn't have as much to do with the inherent goodness of the Chevrolet as the inherent badness of the competition.

Chrysler Corporation had always prided itself on its reputation for engineering excellence. In the early days Chrysler really had been an innovator but by the 1940s the innovations were few and far between. For 1958, that was going to change. Stuff like torsion bar front suspension, outboard rear springs, 3-speed automatic transmission, all-new wider, lower bodies with long canted tailfins designed-in, not tacked on. Station wagons would have permanent, folding, rear facing third seats with spare tires behind an access door in the right rear quarter panel. The tailgate glass would roll down as opposed to swinging up. Station wagons, including Plymouth, would have a wheelbase of 122 inches. While development was progressing at a reasonable pace for the planned 1958 launch, the internal intelligence machine dug up some unsettling news: Ford, Mercury, Oldsmobile, Buick, and Cadillac would be all new for 1957. That would leave Lincoln with a carryover 1956 body and Chevrolet, Pontiac and all Chrysler lines getting a third year out of the 1955 bodies. The decision was made to move the 1958 models up to 1957. There weren't enough job shops in Detroit to tool those cars that fast. Virtually any Detroit area tool and die guy that had room in his garage and was willing to moonlight could become a job shop overnight. When everything came together for the pre-production build, nothing actually came together. It was panic time. Guys with mallets were beating everything into submission. What had started out as a program that would renew Chrysler's engineering reputation was totally wrecked by the production people at the misguided direction of upper management.

Many owners of 1957 Plymouths wished that water would leak out of the trunk as fast as it leaked in. It was comforting to know that the warm red glow of the oil pressure light would always be there, even if all other dash lighting failed. Owners established a tight relationship with the boys down at the transmission shop. The torsion bar pockets were not well sealed allowing slush and salt to creep in. One night, as the car rested (and rusted) in the driveway, there would be a BANG! And everyone would rush out to see the Plymouth kneeling down on one front corner. It was time for a new torsion bar. About a week later, two weeks tops, the other one would snap. The bodies rusted with a vengeance. Even in mild climates, waterlogged carpet padding caused the floors to rust to the point where the front seat fell through the floor before the payment book ran out of coupons.

And then there was Ford. Ford's slide into indifferent quality over the past few years was about to accelerate to outright disaster in 1957. Like Chrysler, Ford had a very ambitious product program for 1957 in which there were, not one, but two Fords on 116 inch and 118 inch wheelbases. The Custom and Custom 300 on the short wheelbase were similar in size to the 115 inch Chevrolet, while the Fairlane and Fairlane 500 were dead on the Plymouth's 118-inch wheelbase but almost a half-foot longer overall. The Fairlane 500 was a big, good looking car with all the gold anodized glitz that any buyer could hope for. Ford had reached all the way up to the middle price class

with the Fairlanes while remaining firmly rooted in the low price field with the Customs. Ford, like Plymouth, was seeing many new faces in the showrooms in 1957, and before long they would be angry faces. They would be the faces of people who hated the flaws in their new Fords and wanted repairs that they weren't getting. As time went by the 1957 Fords proved themselves to be considerably more trouble-prone than their mediocre predecessors. Overhead oiling was notoriously ineffective and rear main seals were a common problem. Fuel pump failures led to contamination of engine oil with resulting bearing failure. Poor fit and finish was a problem in the showroom. Rust was, of course, taken for granted in those days, but some cars were worse than others and the 1957 Fords fit nicely in that category. Riding qualities deteriorated rapidly and too many of those Fords felt too old, too soon. Chevrolet was selling a somewhat smaller, rather dated car compared to the 1957 competition. As a result, Ford outsold Chevrolet and Plymouth regained third place in sales. Chevrolet was building a car, which by its third year, had the greatest portion of the quality bugs worked out. A car whose genetic flaws had surfaced in prior years and were resolved. Well, except Turboglide which was, luckily, a low volume item. It was a car whose plants were operating at below capacity and that can contribute to good quality ratings. So, while the 1957 Chevrolet was a hard sell in 1957, it became a hot used car. Ford and Plymouth owners told their sad story to anybody who would listen. When a Chevy owner was asked what he thought of his car he most likely said something like "been a good car." Eventually this word of mouth evolved into common knowledge and a four-year-old Bel Air was worth twice as much as a four-year-old Belvedere at wholesale level. Because of their extremely high resale value, 1957 Chevrolets were not allowed to die. Only the worst examples were junked when traded-in. The average or better cars were wholesaled to smaller dealers who, in effect, restored them and sent them back in the world as "sharp" used cars. How ironic it was that Chrysler and Ford worked so hard to create cars so desirable that they sold in huge quantities to people who would never again consider their products. Chevrolet, simply by not building a bad car, wound up with icon status.

'55

The **1955 Bel Air Sport Coupe** which became the 50,000,000th GM automobile had 716 trim parts which were gold plated. The gold plated pieces in this layout were "extras" to be used in the event that a part was damaged while assembling, transporting or exhibiting the unique "Golden Chevrolet."

1955: Shoebox styling; 'hot' new V-8

America's youth had heard that there would be a new Chevrolet for 1955 and they had heard that it would have a V-8. Not just a V-8 but a hot V-8. This was good news because a lot of the kids knew that they would never get Dad out of a Chevy and they pined for the kind of performance their friends were getting out of their father's Olds 88 or Hemi Dodge. The new 1954 Fords were out there with the Y-Block V-8 but at 239 cid. They weren't much more worrisome than the Flathead of 1953 and before. In fact, the Ford I-Block six was a pretty good challenger for the V-8. The stick shift and overdrive Fords were gutsy enough but those Ford-O-Matics were below the expectations of those who had been watching Oldsmobile 88s since 1949. These car-savvy young folks were also aware that Ford was supposed to be new for 1955 as well as Plymouth.

In as much as Plymouth had shown nothing in the way of either performance or styling in recent years, very few were expecting much from that quarter. Since Ford's styling had been somewhat more popular with the younger crowd for the last few years, and since Ford already had an OHV V-8 with which to work, many expected 1955 to be a Ford year.

It wasn't like General Motors was caught by surprise by this swing to high compression OHV V-8s. On no, in fact, they started it. In 1949 the Cadillac and Oldsmobile had fired the first shots in the battle to go fast. And, yes, General Motors really did know what a fast car could do for a division's reputation. Before 1949, Oldsmobile had been thought of as an engineer's car. It was the first car to feature the fully automatic Hydra-Matic in 1940. But it was not an exciting kind of car. It just sat there with its chrome and looked middle class. The Rocket engine changed all that, and fast. The beauty was that it could still look middle class and the old Olds fans continued to think of it as the symbol of engineering excellence within General Motors — and they continued to buy.

So let's not think that GM or Chevrolet was caught unprepared by the horsepower race. They may, however, have reacted rather slowly to the emergence of youth as buyers or influencers of the purchase decisions of others. By 1952 though, the corporation began to worry about a future that found even fewer young buyers in Chevrolet showrooms. True, there was a V-8 under development at Chevrolet but it didn't show much promise of catching the eye of youth and

The enlarged "V" in the "Corvette" front fender script identifies this Corvette as a 1955 V-8.

turning the division's image around. This engine was basically a scaled-down version of the 1949 Cadillac engine. Not that there was anything wrong with the 331 cid Cadillac engine, but the idea of using that 1949 technology and reducing it to the planned 230-cid package didn't seem to smack of the type of fresh and innovative thinking that would be required for the image turnaround that the corporate brass had in mind for Chevrolet. Besides, it looked like it was going to be prohibitively expensive to produce.

So it came to pass that an engineer named Ed Cole who had been largely responsible for that 1949 Cadillac OHV V-8 was moved from the Cleveland tank plant in May of 1952 to Chevrolet where he would be chief engineer. Cole immediately reviewed all product plans for 1955 and concluded that the best plan would be to start over with a clean sheet. As the heart of the important new vehicle, he envisioned a lightweight, inexpensive engine designed to take advantage of the latest manufacturing techniques. As it turned out, recently developed casting and manufacturing techniques that were employed to produce this engine were as important as the engine design itself. It was only through the use of these techniques that the new engine could be produced at a reasonable cost. The block was so well done that, as this is being written, nearly 50 years later, it is still the mainstay of GM V-8 engines. The initial displacement, as built in 1955, was 265 cid but it has since been opened up all the way to 400 cid and many sizes between. The new engine design incorporated an innovative and inexpensive valve train design that eliminated the rocker shafts and

replaced the traditional cast rocker arms with lightweight stamped arms. Further weight savings were realized with hollow push rods and the elimination of the stamped valley cover. The inlet manifold was bolted to the heads and doubled to serve the function of the no longer needed separate cover. The design efficiency of this engine can best be appreciated when we realize that V-8-equipped cars weighed 40 to 60 pounds less than six-cylinder models. At introduction the horsepower rating was 162. This was soon joined by a power pack option, which combined a four-barrel carburetor and dual exhaust for 180 horsepower. Near the end of the model year, the Corvette version of the 265 was made available in all passenger cars.

While the new V-8 was certainly the big news for 1955, the 235-cid six was still very important in the overall picture. At 123 horsepower with manual shift models and 136 horses with Powerglide, the new Chevy sixes moved the light bodies (a 150 two-door weighed just 3,060 pounds) along very briskly. When we consider that the 1955 Chevrolet six-cylinder with Powerglide was rated at 136 horses and that the 1954 Ford Y-Block V-8 developed only 130 horses, it becomes apparent that Chevrolet was serious about delivering performance across the board.

The 1955 Chevrolet was about much more than just an engine. It was truly an all-new car. From the frame up, including the frame, the suspension, the entire driveline, the body and just about everything attached to any of the above. The old standby, torque

You are looking at the last word in architecture for a smaller dealership in 1955. The showroom display includes a 210 four-door sedan and a 210 four-door station wagon as well as a second-series pickup.

tube drive, was replaced by Hotchkiss drive. According to the 1955 Chevrolet Features book from October, 1954, the Hotchkiss drive "permits a more desirable design throughout the entire power train. The influence of this basic change is manifested in a completely different dynamic character of the car, of a type usually associated with far heavier, more expensive cars." The design provided "increased driveline smoothness, easier handling and reduced weight and permitted a lower silhouette."

The new frame was shaped from tubular stock. Again quoting from the Features book: "The box girder frame is fifty percent more rigid and more than eighteen percent lighter." To this innovative new frame Chevrolet engineers attached new front and rear suspension. It is interesting to note that the Features book refers to the new front suspension as "Knee-Action Suspension" while describing the combined features, particularly spherical joints, (ball joints) that result in an exclusive innovation, "braking dive control." It was stated that brake dive was reduced approximately 45 percent. The new steering system was said to provide "reduced steering effort, greater operating smoothness, and increased durability." The new steering was of the recirculating ball and nut type previously used only with power steering equipped Chevrolets. Clutch and brake pedals were now suspended, a feature pioneered by Ford in 1952. The brake master cylinder moved to a much more convenient location under the hood. The parking brake "T" handle was relocated from the right side of the steering column to the left side. Tubeless tires were

introduced as standard equipment for 1955. The wheels were closely monitored for rim bead seal finish and weld finish to assure a tight seal. Four small stamped lugs were added to the outside horizontal portion of the rim to aid in the retention of the full wheelcovers. The series designations of 1953 and 1954 — 150, 210 and Bel Air — were continued for 1955. Internally, the Bel Air was known as the 2400 Series and initially included the four-door sedan, two-door sedan, Sport Coupe, convertible and four-door station wagon. The Bel Air line was soon expanded to include the Nomad, an innovative premium two-door station wagon whose styling was based on a Corvette show car.

The more affordable 210 series (internally designated series 2100) was expanded to include a pillarless Sport Coupe (available in 1953 but missing in 1954) and a two-door station wagon along with the familiar four-door sedan, Delray Club Coupe, two-door sedan, and four-door station wagon. While identified as a Club Coupe, the Delray was externally identical to the two-door sedan. Inside, it had a dramatically different look with two-tone vinyl upholstery sewn in a biscuit pattern and carpet replacing the two-door sedan's rubber mat. The two-door station wagon, like all 1955 Chevrolet wagons, was rated for six-passengers.

The fleet-oriented 150 series (known internally as series 1500) was slightly re-arranged with a two-door station wagon replacing the previous four-door model. Continued were the four-door sedan, two-door sedan, three-passenger Utility Sedan, and Sedan

This auto show display features a V-8 Corvette, a convertible with continental kit, a Nomad, a Bel Air Station Wagon and a Bel Air four-door sedan.

Delivery. The utility sedan was, of course, the modern equivalent of the business coupe and shared the two-door body shell. The most popular offering in the 1955 Chevrolet line was the Bel Air four-door sedan with better than 345,000 units sold. The runner-up was the 210 four-door sedan at almost 318,000. Today's collector favorites, the Bel Air Sport Coupe and Convertible, sold more than 185,000 and more than 41,000 vehicles, respectively. The unique and beautiful Nomad sold just over 6,000 copies, making it quite rare by Chevrolet volume standards.

At the low end of the market there had always been some demand for no-frills basic transportation vehicles to fill the needs of fleet users, buyers who just wanted a reliable way to get from point A to point B, and those who needed to stay within a tight budget. It was those buyers who drove away with a little over 125,000 150 series cars in 1955 (excluding sedan deliveries). The best selling 150 was the two-door sedan. Using that model as a comparison base, it cost buyers just 90 1955 dollars to move up to a comparable 210. For that money the buyer got a color-keyed interior utilizing nicer fabrics, color-keyed rubber floor mats, upgraded door trim panels, ashtrays, armrests, glovebox light, horn ring, windshield and backlight moldings, belt moldings, rear quarter moldings and more. Of course, 1955 dollars were big, value-packed dollars but the move to the 210 at just 90 of those dollars seems to have been quite a bargain. Somewhere over 806,000 buyers agreed and they made the 210 Chevrolet's most popular series. In a close second place finish at almost 771,000 was the

stylish Bel Air series. Again using the two-door sedan as a comparison base, the Bel Air was a $113 step-up from the 210. For that premium the buyer received carpets, upgraded fabrics and interior trim design, additional instrument panel trim, front fender and door moldings, upper door and pillar moldings, full wheel covers, Bel Air scripts, crests and more. At this point, the Chevrolet buyer, at least visually, if not financially, crossed into territory that was historically occupied by names like Buick, Olds, and De Soto. In fact, in the author's opinion, the 1955 Bel Air was a more visually impressive product than a Buick Special, Buick Century, De Soto Firedome or Chrysler Windsor. While it still didn't feel or drive like those up-market cars, it did manage to out-class them in terms of interior opulence.

The 1955 Corvette made very good use of the new V-8 engine although a few early cars were produced with the Blue Flame six. The V-8, as utilized by Corvette, was rated at 195 horsepower with a Rochester four-barrel carburetor. The 12-volt ignition system of full-size Chevrolets was incorporated, as was an automatic choke. These would be the first Chevrolets to feature electric windshield wipers as standard equipment. The Powerglide automatic continued to be the only transmission available until late in the model year when the three-speed manual appeared. While never really slow, it could be said that the Corvette was now really fast. From the outside it was not possible to tell a 1954 Corvette from a 1955 Corvette with a six-cylinder engine. The V-8s were easier. The "V" in the front fender nameplate was

This Bel Air four-door sedan has a clear plastic hood to display the engine and the under hood portion of new air conditioning system.

enlarged, providing instant engine and model year identification. During the year Harvest Gold with green trim, Corvette Copper and Gypsy Red were phased in while Pennant Blue and Sportsman Red were discontinued. Ford launched the two-passenger Thunderbird. The Thunderbird was aimed at the "personal use market" while the Corvette was being marketed as a sports car. Many of the experts of the day snubbed the 1953 and 1954 Corvette for a number of reasons, not the least of which was that Powerglide transmission. The frequent criticism was that it just wasn't a sports car. The V-8 and standard transmission went a long way toward negating that criticism.

Whatever the domestic two-seater market may have been called in 1955 it seemed to like the Thunderbird, which got off to a good start, better than the Corvette which had a dismal year. It would be next year before the Corvette got the credit and sales it deserved in 1955.

So what about the traditional competition? Well, Ford had a nice car. A facelift that was so well done that most buyers thought their 1955 Ford was an all-new car. It wasn't but the new wraparound windshield combined with new exterior body panels and new interior styling to effectively provide an all-new look. The new Fairlane series replaced the Crestline of 1954 to compete directly with the Bel Air. While Bel Air sedan interiors tended to be more stylish, Fairlane interiors looked to be a bit more luxurious. This year Ford introduced the Crown Victoria, one of the least logical body styles in history. After half a decade in

which the industry promoted, and charged a premium price for the two-door hardtop body style in which the center pillar was deleted, Ford took a premium price Victoria, added a center pillar to create a tarty two-door sedan and bumped up the price. More than 33,000 buyers took the bait and another 2,000 plunked down an additional $70 for a Plexiglas front roof section that turned the glitzy thing into a rolling solarium. Barnum would have loved it!

The Ford Customline was a direct competitor for the Chevrolet 210. Pricing was similar with the Ford, which was priced $26 above the Chevrolet based on two-door sedan comparisons. The trim levels were similar but Ford may have gained a slight edge with a full-length body side molding vs. the Chevy's rear quarter molding. There was no hardtop in the Customline series to compete with the 210 Sport Coupe. There was also no direct competitor for the Delray. Ford's Mainline series was the entry-level competition for the 150. Like the 150 it was very basic and geared to the fleet market. The Mainline was available in two-door and four-door sedan versions as well as a business coupe which shared the two-door sedan body shell and wasn't really a coupe. The Mainline with a little over 127,000 units was slightly more popular than the 150 reflecting Ford's historic strength at the very bottom of the market. Ford had always been strong in the station wagon market and in 1955 began to market the wagons as a separate series with the two-door Ranch Wagon at the Mainline trim level, the Custom Ranch Wagon and the four-door Country Sedan at the Customline trim level and the

This clear plastic hood reveals the under hood air conditioning components. Compare the size of that compressor with a modern unit. Also seen are power brakes, power steering, and the power pack setup with four-barrel carburetor.

woodgrained Country Squire at the Fairlane trim level. Ford had a good handle on the wagon market and offered both six- and nine-passenger models in 1955 while Chevrolet offered only six-passenger wagons. It should come as no surprise that Ford's wagons outsold Chevy wagons by a margin of about three to two.

Chrysler Corporation was losing ground in the early 1950s. The conservative leadership of K.T. Keller, a former Chevrolet production man, had resulted in vehicles that were falling below consumer expectations in several areas including styling and, more recently, quality. While the more expensive Chrysler and De Soto had maintained fairly high standards, the bodies of the 1953 and 1954 Plymouth and Dodge were tinny, flimsy, poorly engineered and haphazardly constructed. Worse yet, many buyers didn't like their stubby appearance. It wasn't until 1954 that they could offer a clutch-less fully automatic transmission. Chrysler had Virgil Exner to lead design but Keller and powerful engineers had repeatedly interfered with his proposed designs resulting in the 1953-54 disaster. Keller finally saw the buyers drifting away and took the chains off Virgil Exner and designer Maurie Baldwin.

The resulting 1955 models were Chrysler's first really good looking cars that decade. The 240-cid V-8 developed 157 horsepower. There were also two 260-cid versions, a two-barrel developing 167 horses and a four-barrel kicking out 177 horses. While looking good on paper these powerplants were still not enough to put Plymouth in Chevy's league. But the long, clean lines were hard to fault. Interior styling was good with

the exception of the odd, symmetrical instrument panel layout that placed the temperature and oil pressure gauges in front of the passenger. Plymouth was the last to offer full instrumentation; Ford and Chevrolet had switched to warning lights.

Plymouth also offered three series; the Belvedere competed with the Bel Air. The mid-level Savoy competed with the 210 and the Plaza was the entry-level competitor for the 150. While the Plaza's exterior trim was as stark as that of the 150 and the Mainline, the color-keyed interiors were nicer to look at. Perhaps that is why the Plaza two-door and four-door sedans outsold the 150 and the Mainline. Plymouth's best seller was the four-door Sedan in the mid-level Savoy line. Even at that the 210 four-door Sedan outsold the Savoy four-door sedan at the rate of two-to-one. The Belvedere was a sportier looking car than its stuffy name would imply. All three Plymouth lines were available with extra-cost Sport Tone moldings which could be used to outline special contrasting paint treatments. Plymouth colors with names like Pompano Peach and Tampa Turquoise were symbolic of the lighthearted and optimistic attitudes of 1955.

When all the numbers were in, Chevrolet had maintained leadership and Ford had enjoyed its second best year-to-date. It is interesting to be able to reflect from the vantage point of many years that the 1955 Chevrolets were actually better, longer-lasting cars than the competitors. While all 1955 cars rusted in the salt belt, the Plymouth generally rusted sooner and worse. The rocker panel and floor areas were more

This new 1955 210 Sport Coupe is wearing a grille guard, outside mirror, gas door guard, radio antenna and whitewalls.

vulnerable than those of Chevrolet and Ford so that critical structural damage occurred very early.

Chevrolet's "magic circle" followed a rubber gasket outlining the rear inner wheel housing resulting in rust perforation forming an arc on the quarter panel, but that didn't happen right away. Ford fenders and quarter panels packed it in fairly early, as did Plymouth's. More important, Chevrolets seemed to be more reliable in old age. A good part of this can be attributed to the Chevrolet's 12-volt electrical system that Ford and Plymouth didn't get until 1956. Ford carburetors got temperamental as time went by. The combination of six-volt electrical system and bad carb aggravated by ring and valve wear made for some very hard-starting Fords! And the eight-cylinder Plymouths were just about as bad. There was also a tendency for these Fords, which were great, solid drivers when new, to get very loose as the miles piled on. The buyers of 1955 couldn't have known about the durability issues when they bought their new cars but a hefty percentage of them made the right long-term decision anyway and selected the Chevrolet, which retained the historic first place with 23 percent of total industry sales. Ford was an easy second place with 22.3 percent. Plymouth rebounded from the 1954 disaster with 9.4 percent of the market, but still finished behind Buick, landing in fourth place.

Late in 1954, General Motors prepared to celebrate a remarkable event; the production of the corporation's 50-millionth vehicle. As in 1940, when the 25-millionth GM vehicle was produced by

Chevrolet, the corporation's highest volume division was, once again, tapped for the honor. The 50-millionth vehicle was to be a specially trimmed 1955 Chevrolet Bel Air Sport Coupe built in Flint. Following an appropriate period of preparatory hype, the gold Sport Coupe body was mated to a gold chassis and rolled down the assembly line at 10 a.m. on November 23, 1954 and joined its 49 million, nine hundred ninety nine thousand, nine hundred ninety nine brothers and sisters. A gold GM Diesel locomotive headed up a trainload of celebrities and invited guests arriving in Flint. Corporate and divisional executives flocked to the assembly plant for speeches and photo opps.

Chevrolet General manager, T.H. Keating, presented the key to GM chairman Harlow Curtis. As the in-plant festivities wound down, number 50 million was loaded on a float and was the star of a gala parade through Flint. Schools were closed for the entire day so that students and teachers could participate in the festivities. Corporate and civic leaders as well as celebrities waved from new GM convertibles to crowds that packed the sidewalks of downtown Flint. Each division (and the UAW) had its own lavish float, AC sent giant marching spark plugs and marching bands from a number of nearby communities made this a proud and memorable day in Flint history. It was all quite symbolic of the values and optimism that typified mid-America in the post-war fifties. It may even have been the all-time high point in Flint's history.

This 1955 auto show shot includes a 210 two-door station wagon, a Nomad and a Bel Air Convertible with continental kit.

The 1955
Corvette V-8
seems to have
a hood fit
problem. That
seems kind of
unusual for an
auto show
display car, but
not that
atypical for
Corvettes of
this vintage.

This milestone — the production of the 32nd-millionth Chevrolet, a '55 Bel Air Convertible — was over-shadowed by the 50,000,000th GM vehicle, which was also a 1955 Chevrolet. Three adults were obviously a tight fit in that narrow rear seat.

In this staged shot the driver of the 1955 Bel Air Convertible is probably having more fun with that puddle than the poor guy on the sidewalk.

The sew pattern and vinyl seats tell us that this 1955 210 two-door is actually a Del Ray Club Coupe.

This 1955 150 station wagon was used by a Berrien County, Michigan representative of Detroit's Goebel Brewery.

This pretty 1955 Bel Air Nomad may not have had the cargo capacity of other '55 Chevrolet wagons, but it sure was a lot prettier.

The rear passenger compartment of a 1955 Chevrolet Bel Air Sport Coupe was a bright and friendly place.

This is a 1955 Chevrolet Bel Air four-door sedan. The whitewalls are the only visible option.

The two-door sedan was the third best seller in the Bel Air series. This one wears a somewhat uncommon single color paint job.

The 1955 150
Sedan Delivery
is shown with
the new style
liftgate in the
upright position.

A newly assembled 1955 210 Sport Coupe is ready to be loaded for shipment to a dealer.

This 1955 Bel Air Sport Coupe was on display at the dealer announcement show. Who wouldn't want that beautiful carpet in their living room?

The new Ferrari-inspired grille is shown on a 1955 210 four-door sedan.

(Right) The date is early 1955, the location is GM's Milford Proving Ground and the spectators are members of the 100 Car Club (Chevrolet salesmen who sold at least 100 cars per year). We are guessing that the dark Corvette is a V-8 prototype and that the salesmen are witnessing a six vs. V-8 drag race.

The little cowgirl is driving Chevrolet's best-selling four-door wagon, the Bel Air Beauville, available only in six-passenger form.

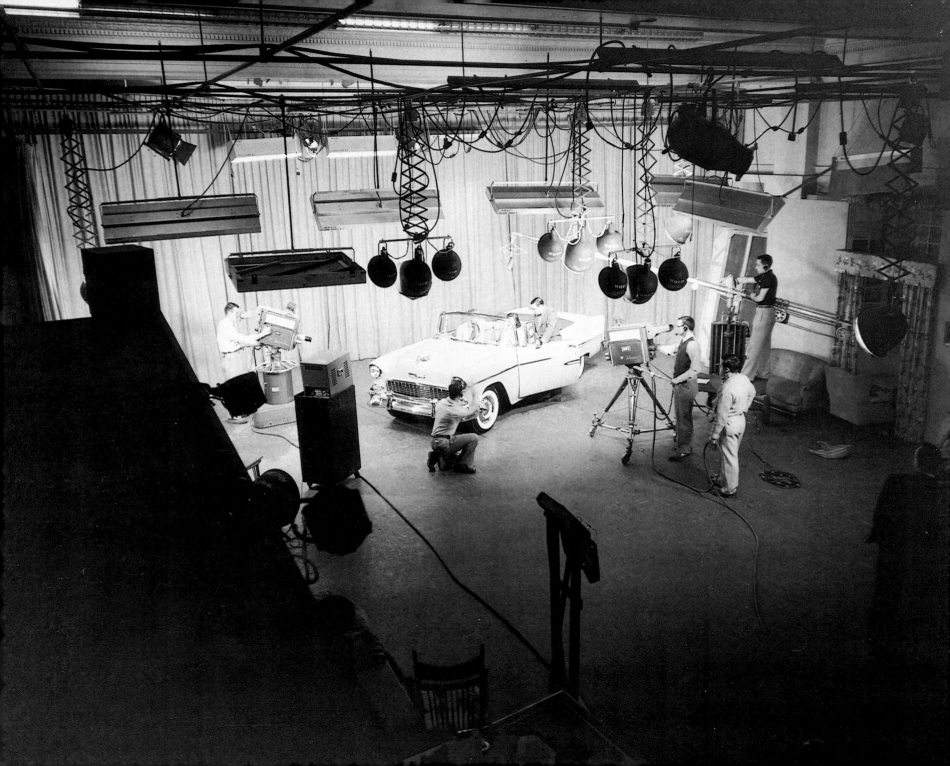

(Left)
The Bel Air Convertible is on the studio set of WQED TV, probably filming a live commercial.

A group of cold GM executives parade through Flint during the 50,000,000th GM car celebration. Look at the beautiful fit on that top boot.

These kids are peddling around in, what are today, some very valuable little cars.

The blackwall tires and dog dish hubcaps aside, this 1955 Belvedere two-door hardtop was Plymouth's best looking car in years. Compare the wraparound windshield treatment to Chevrolet and Ford.

This is the front compartment of a 1955 Chevrolet 210. Note the rubber floor mat and lack of instrument panel trim. This vehicle has a day/night mirror.

The 1955 Ford Customline was competitive with the 210. The front fender emblem indicates an I-Block six-cylinder is living under the hood.

At this angle, the Chevy 150 four-door sedan looks very different from the 210 and Bel Air models. The lack of trim makes the mid-section look longer and the front and rear appear shorter.

Study this one carefully. This is a Canadian Chevy 150 four-door sedan. The side trim is similar to that used on a 210 Station Wagon. When this trim is combined with full wheel covers the car looks much more upscale than the U.S. version.

This is the front compartment of a 1955 Bel Air Sport Coupe. This one was loaded with Powerglide, power windows, power brakes, signal-seeking radio, rear speaker, parking brake signal, heater and day/night mirror. Note the bow-tie pattern in the instrument panel trim.

The interior of the 1955 Canadian 150, which incorporated the 210 steering wheel, had a more upscale appearance than the U.S. version.

The roomy trunk of the 1955 Bel Air Sedan featured smooth side walls and a durable mat.

'55

The driver of this 1955 210 Del Ray Club Coupe has stopped to allow a train to pass across the studio floor. Although named Club Coupe, it shares the 210 two-door sedan body.

Except for the whitewalls and two-tone paint, this 210 four-door sedan is without visible options.

The 1955 Bel Air four-door sedan was a well-dressed car, even when in base condition, like this one whose whitewalls are the only visible options.

This might have been America's most recognizable profile in 1955. The Nomad was a tremendous advance in station wagon styling if not practicality.

This 1955 Sedan Delivery shows off the new lift gate. This prototype rides a little higher in the rear than production models.

The bright roof bows and beautiful waffle pattern vinyl interior made the 1955 Nomad a great place to be. Note the radio blockout panel, which was used until the dealer installed a radio.

A proud Ed Cole poses with a 1955 Bel Air Sport Coupe in the Chevrolet lobby on the first floor of the GM Building annex. Cole was Chevrolet's chief engineer at the time. He became general manager of Chevy in 1956.

The 1955 150 four-door sedan looked less severe when equipped with whitewalls.

This was Chevrolet's lowest-priced six-passenger 1955 model, the 150 two-door sedan in completely base condition.

Linoleum trimmed with bright metal covered the cargo floor and combined with two-tone vinyl to create a bright cheerful interior in the 1955 Bel Air Beauville Station Wagon.

The 1955 Bel Air Beauville was a four-door station wagon for six passengers. There were no three-seat wagons from Chevrolet in 1955.

At first we thought the driver had popped a wheelie while demonstrating the startling acceleration of his new 1955 Bel Air convertible with 265 V-8. We now tend to believe the car was hung from the ceiling. Honest.

In this seldom seen angle we can view the upholstery pattern in a 1955 Bel Air Convertible.

With nosy neighbors like these we can understand why the owner of the 1955 Bel Air four-door sedan put up that wall. She also elected to buy whitewalls and two-tone paint.

This is the patterned cloth interior of a 1955 Bel Air four-door sedan. Note the integral armrest design exclusive to the Bel Air trim level.

The sleek lines of the 1955 Bel Air Sport Coupe are well displayed in this view. The small "V" emblems below the taillights indicate a V-8 engine.

This 1955 265 V-8 is equipped with power steering. The power steering pump is on the rear of the generator.

Top down and looking great, this 1955 Bel Air Convertible is obviously pleasing the three pretty occupants.

Whitewalls and two-tone paint are the only visible options on this 1955 Bel Air Sport Coupe.

This 1955 210 four-door sedan is a six-cylinder as evidenced by the lack of "V" emblems under the taillights.

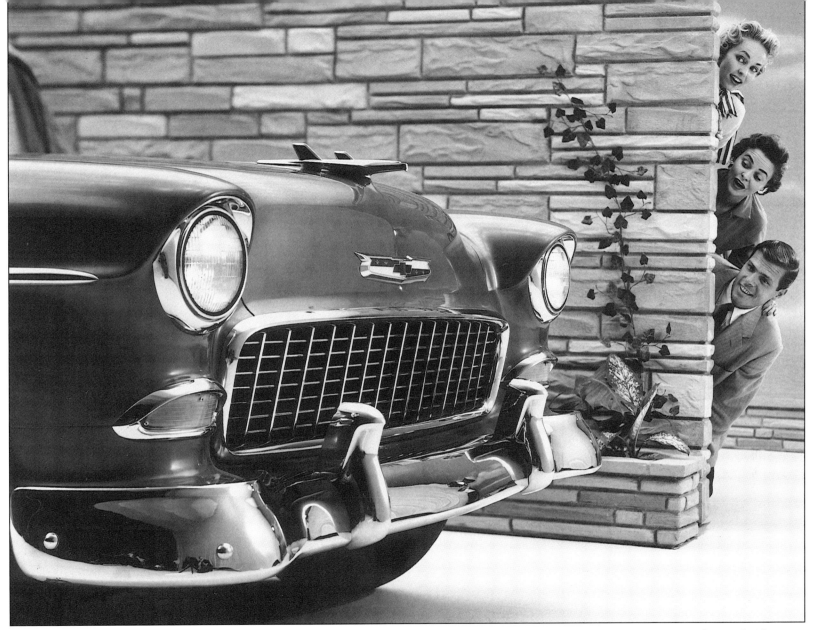

The controversial front end of the 1955 Chevrolet is shown at its best in this dramatic close-up of a Bel Air.

While not exactly luxurious, the 1955 150 four-door sedan was appropriate for its price class with patterned cloth and vinyl. The floor mat was black rubber for easy maintenance.

The Duke of Windsor was a fan of GM products. This 1955 210 Townsman Station Wagon was modified for him. Note the bars over the rear quarter windows to prevent damage from shifting cargo.

Special door pockets were among the custom touches on the 1955 210 Townsman Station Wagon built for the Duke of Windsor.

These protective bars were applied over the windows of the Duke of Windsor's 1955 210 Townsman Station Wagon to protect them from shifting cargo.

DAWSON
5-20-53

7743

This proposal for a 1955 210 four-door sedan was photographed on May 20, 1953. The front end was rather Ford-like.

The high crease across the back of this 1955 proposal contributed to a high, narrow look. This image was taken on May 20, 1953.

The front gravel pan of this 1955 Bel Air Sport Coupe has been chromed and the inside surfaces of the grille have been painted body color. The vehicle has a spotlight.

Two historic vehicles here. The 1955 Bel Air is the 50,000,000th GM car; the 1940 Special Deluxe Sport Sedan is the 25,000,000th GM car. The 1940 is still owned by GM. The 1955 got away.

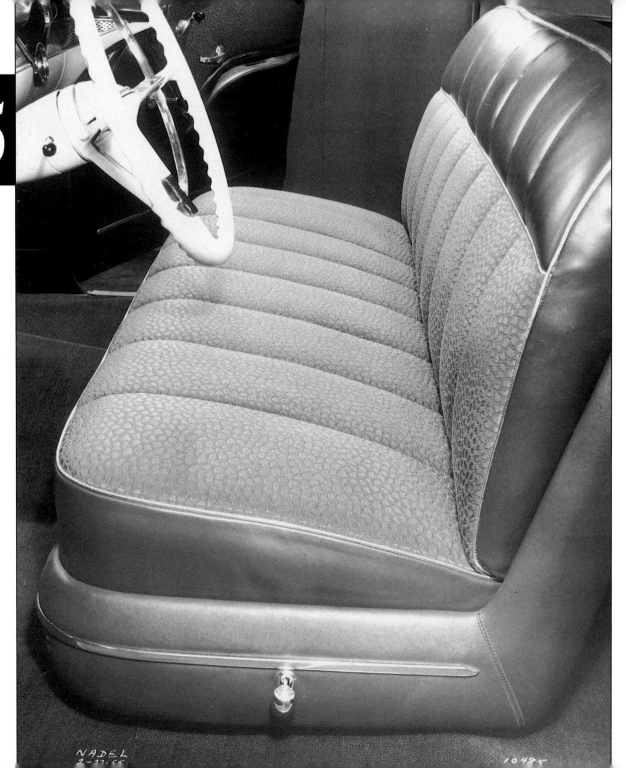

This special interior was installed in a 1955 Bel Air for a VIP. It was somewhat reminiscent of those found in Oldsmobile 98s of that era.

(Right)

Take a close look at this 1955 Chevrolet 150 test mule. Did you notice the 1953 grille?

The sculptor is working on a clay model of a 1955 Bel Air Sport Coupe which will become a model for 24 foot fiberglass models to be used on bigger than life 3-D billboards in Detroit and several other cities.

Here's that beautiful rear end with seven stripes on the tailgate. The blackwall tires certainly detract from the appearance.

This pleated leather interior was installed in Harley Earl's personal Nomad. While beautiful and luxurious it lacks the classic appeal of the standard two-tone waffle pattern vinyl interior. Earl, of course, was vice president of styling for General Motors.

This interior was installed in the Bel Air Sport Coupe of Thomas Keating, general manager of Chevrolet.

This 1955 Bel Air Convertible was used by Dinah Shore during a personal appearance. The singer was a Chevrolet spokesperson in the 1950s and was known for singing the commercial jingle, "See the U.S.A. in your Chevrolet ..."

(Left)
A very pretty
1955 Nomad
arrives at the
end of the
assembly line.

A Texas dealer used this 1955 210 four-door sedan to demonstrate the newly available air conditioning. Note the grille guard, fender guards, sunvisor, sill molding and more. Strangely, standard hubcaps were used in combination with all the other goodies.

The Chevrolet Biscayne, a four-door hardtop with suicide rear doors was new on the show car circuit in 1955. More than 30 years later this car was hauled out of a Michigan junkyard and restored.

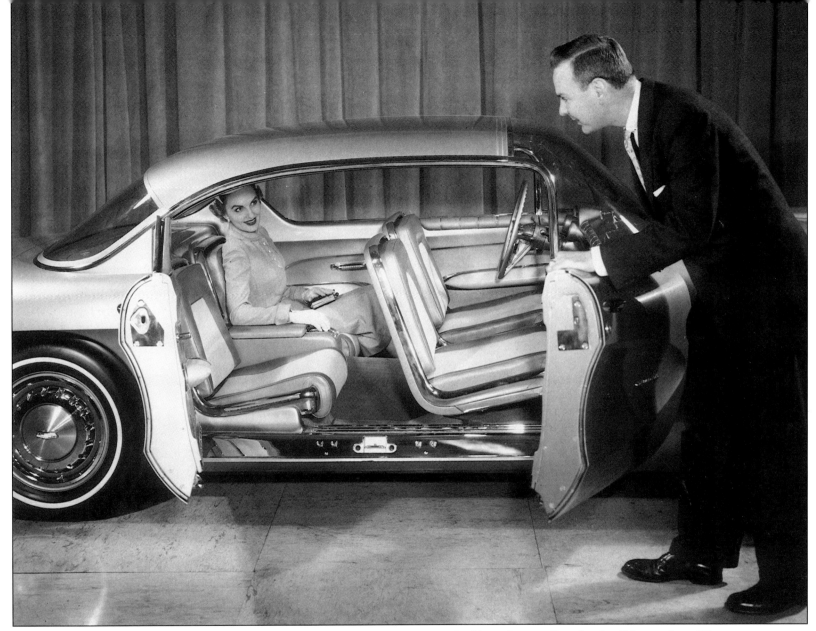

The Biscayne show car of 1955 had many unique features including doors that locked into the sills, eliminating the center post for ease of entry to the individual rear seats. Note the rear console.

(Right)
The Nomad is missing but the rest of the Bel Air line is present for this family portrait. The two-door sedan looks rather odd without whitewalls.

Air conditioning created a great deal of underhood clutter in 1955.

A Bel Air convertible, 210 two-door with fender guards and a Bel Air four-door sedan are shown at a 1955 auto show.

This 1955 Bel Air has air conditioning, Wonder Bar radio, rear speaker spotlight, tissue dispenser, compass and day/night mirror.

We don't know the significance of the numbers on the windshields but we recognize the 1955 Bel Air and the 1941 Special Deluxe which, at this time, was just a 14 year old used car.

We don't see many shots of early Corvettes with blackwall tires, but that's the case with this 1955 V-8. The helmeted driver must have been doing some fancy driving at this event. He appears to be Indy winner and GM employee Maury Rose.

This shot of the 1955 Indy 500 official pace car appears to have been taken at an airport. Whoever was arriving (or leaving) rated a band in addition to this prestigious transportation.

This art proposal from Campbell-Ewald, Chevrolet's ad agency, was the basis for a number of huge billboards with a 3-D representation of a larger-than-life 1955 Bel Air Sport Coupe.

The 1955 Chevrolet Biscayne show car featured this instrument panel. Stock switches and steering wheel were used but the entire horn ring assembly was chromed. Attractive but probably annoying on a sunny day.

EVANS
9-23-53

8058

A full-size blackboard drawing from 1953 reveals that some consideration was given to a 1955 El Camino. The 210 trim level was represented and 1954 wheelcovers were illustrated.

The notation on the envelope for this 1955 Corvette proposal indicated that this was an approved design as late as March, 1954. Note that there are two different headlamp designs. That hood scoop may have been a response to the T-Bird.

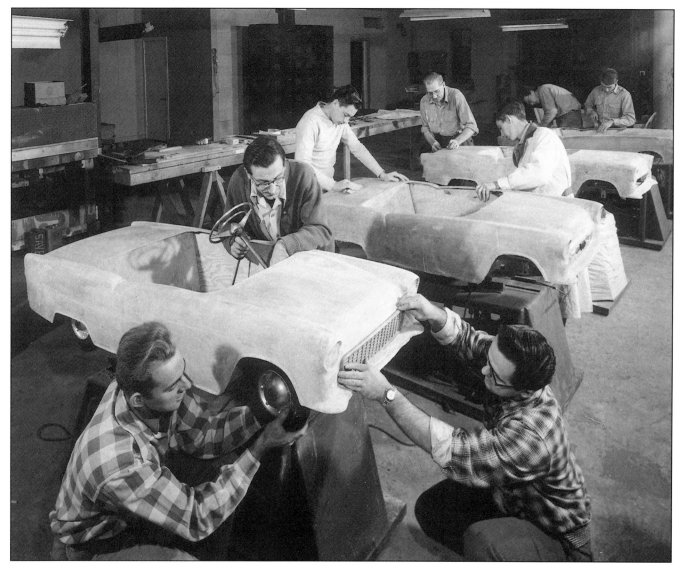

(Left)
All General
Motors
products were
represented at
the 1955
Motorama.
Show cars
were displayed
on individual
turntables
clustered
around the
stage. The
Chevrolet
Biscayne is at
the upper left
with the rear
door open.

While not quite the type of assembly line employed in the production of the full-size 1955 Chevrolets, the 1955 Chevrolet Kiddie Convertibles were also mass-produced.

A 1955 210 Sport Coupe with six-cylinder engine is about to leave the assembly line.

A 1955 Bel Air four-door sedan is riding very low, possibly because it was carrying a load of test equipment associated with the device attached to the rear bumper. The man in the back seat appears to be operating the control console.

In 1954 Thomas Keating was the general manager of the Chevrolet Motor Division. He is shown with the 50,000,000th General Motors car. The gold 1955 Bel Air Sport Coupe was produced in November of 1954. The bright trim was gold plated. Note that the interior also differed from production.

This 1955 210 Townsman four-door station wagon looks right at home in suburbia with mom and the kids. It's a V-8 with whitewalls and a radio.

This is the prototype build of a 1955 Bel Air Sedan with overdrive. The financial folks wanted this divided windshield but, in the end the sales and styling guys prevailed with a one-piece windshield. The temporary floor mat is made of industrial-grade rubber. A close look reveals that an outside sunvisor has been fitted.

This staged shot shows a group of Chevrolet stylists in a simulated studio environment. The car on the blackboard is a 53-54 Corvette (no big "V" in the side script) while the real car is a 1955 Bel Air Sport Coupe.

This is the interior of a 1955 210 Handyman two-door station wagon. The two-tone vinyl interior was color-keyed.

This is the rear compartment of a 1955 210 four-door sedan. This view shows the pattern of the rubber floor carpet.

This two-tone 1955 Bel Air V-8 convertible has whitewalls and no other extra-cost items. The top is a bit puckered around the quarter window.

This is the 1956 Bel Air Sport Sedan used in the Pike's Peak hill climb on September 9, 1955. The technician is holding a false fender cap that will be part of the camouflage package.

A technician is installing false front fender caps to disguise the Pike's Peak hill climb 1956 Bel Air Sport Sedan.

1956:
The 'hot' one gets hotter

The domestic auto industry was on a roll in 1956. Exciting new products in 1955 had left many divisions flush with success. They were feasting. Famine was a reality to others who were not so fortunate. Packard was on the ropes and this would be the last year for the "real" Packard although there would be two more years of Studebaker based, badge engineered, Packards. The bigger Nash and Hudson were doomed to disappear in two years and Kaiser and Willys were already gone.

Chevrolet had launched a successful new car in 1955 and was determined to do more of the things that made 1955 a good year. The theme for 1956 was "The Hot One's Even Hotter." And, indeed, it was. Chevrolet had entered racing in a big way in 1955, attracting drivers like Marshall Teague who had helped put the

now defunct step-down Hudsons on the map. It was like a gift from heaven for Chevrolet to find several good racing teams who had been stranded when the "real" Hudson was dropped at the end of the 1954 model year. They also quietly hired some of Hudson's key inside support staff to coordinate the racing program.

Determined to keep up the momentum fueled by racing successes, Chevrolet kicked off the 1956 model year with another performance bombshell; the Pike's Peak record run. Since 1953 Chevrolet had employed Zora Arkus-Duntov, an engineer with an extensive background in sports car racing. It was decided that Duntov would run a 1956 Chevrolet up Pike's Peak in an attack on a 20-year-old record that had been set by Cannonball Baker. Chevrolet carefully arranged all details to gain the most publicity as well as credibility. Bill France's NASCAR was selected to sanction the event, which took place on September 9, 1955.

Duntov sprinted up the 12.5-mile course and was greeted 17 minutes and 24.05 seconds later at the end of the run by his wife and a group of jubilant Chevrolet officials and NASCAR observers. The old record had been broken by two minutes. Duntov then scampered down the mountain, climbed in another 1956 Chevrolet and sped back to the peak, this time taking 17 minutes and 41.91 seconds. Yes, there were two 1956 Chevrolet Bel Airs involved, one of the new Sport Sedans and a regular post four-door sedan. Both were powered by the 205-horsepower V-8 and both were run up the mountain that day, each breaking the old record. Because the date of these runs was well over a month

The once beautiful 1956 Bel Air Sport Sedan has been very effectively disguised with wide bands of flat paint and phony panel extensions. The rear quarter panel extension is reminiscent of an Aero Willys while the front and side look a bit like a 1956 Packard Executive.

ahead of announcement day, the cars were disguised with fiberglass fender and quarter panel extensions and broad horizontal black and white paint bands that ran completely around the car. It took some guts to introduce your new car to the public in that condition but it was just too early to reveal the styling details.

Chevrolet had film crews on the mountain and, by the November announcement day, a promotional theatrical, "Colorado Climax," was being shown to theatre audiences across the country to publicize Chevrolet's new found performance image. And Chevrolet was making the necessary product improvements to reinforce that image. The base 235-cid six was now good for 140 horsepower. The base 265-cid "Turbo-Fire" V-8 was still rated at 162 horsepower but Powerglide models were now turning out 170 horses. The "power pack" 265 jumped to 205 horsepower. In January, Chevrolet turned up the volume again by offering, in all passenger cars, a dual four-barrel version of the Corvette engine which pushed the horsepower up to 225. These were truly wild times in which most of the manufacturers were involved in the horsepower race and each kept raising the ante as if in an automotive-based poker game. And the stakes were high — the hearts and wallets of the buying public.

Chevrolet made a full-fledged assault on the NASCAR Speedweek at Daytona Beach and came home with a truckload of honors, winning more individual classes and setting more individual records than any other car in its price class. Chevrolet's "The Sales Promoter," Volume 2 number 2, put it this way: "Chevrolet set a new speed record in the flying mile — taking first and second spots, and six out of the top ten places. Chevy was also a record-breaking winner in the acceleration test, taking nine out of the first ten places." Corvette also did well: "The Corvette took the first two places in the flying mile for U.S. Production Sports Cars — won the acceleration run for modified sports cars." Although beyond the scope of this book, even the Chevrolet truck came in for honors: "A modified Cameo Carrier set astonishing new truck records by winning special runs in acceleration and the flying mile."

Then as now, Chevrolet's top performance car was the Corvette. Introduced as an American sports car in 1953, the Corvette had not hit its mark. The Blue Flame six coupled with Powerglide had failed to ignite flames of passion in sports car buyers in 1953 and 1954. The advent of V-8 power and availability of a three-speed manual shift in 1955 got Corvette some respect but even fewer buyers, just 700.

Chevrolet and GM were accustomed to big volumes and Corvette was looking more like a failure than a prestige item. Of course, it was Harley Earl's baby and Corvette, in a vastly improved form, was back for 1956. Just about everything about the Corvette was improved for 1956. The most easily noticed thing was the styling. While not a completely new body, it would have been hard not to like it. The front fenders thrust forward aggressively while the rear quarters tapered smoothly downward with taillights recessed in near-horizontal chrome pods.

The body of the Pike's Peak Bel Air Sport Sedan was given a coat of dull black paint with contrasting stripes. Fender skirts were added and later removed.

The tailpipes were moved outboard and now exited through the tips of the quarter panels directly below the taillights. Twin air scoops, like those on the original Motorama show car, were perched on the front fenders ahead of the windshield. An elliptic recessed cove flowed back from the front wheel opening through the fender and most of the door. The convertible top was redesigned to alleviate the "bubble" look that had characterized earlier models. A sleek new removable hardtop was offered for use with or without the folding top. No longer recessed, the license plate was now mounted below the trunk lid. The grille was slightly elongated with the ends squared off a bit. The wheelcovers and simulated knockoff hubs were redesigned for a more muscular look. The passenger compartment refinements were of a similar magnitude. While the instrument panel was largely carryover, the new steering wheel screamed "sports car" and new seat and door panel designs were executed in a distinctive waffle pattern vinyl. More important, the plug-in windows were replaced by the convenient roll-up type. It is likely that most viewers thought that this was an all-new car and certainly many of them lusted for it.

In 1955 the Corvette and Ford's Thunderbird were two-passenger cars, directed at different markets. Although early Ford documents called the T-Bird a sports car, they soon decided it was really a "personal car." In 1956 each vehicle moved closer to their own intended market and farther from each other. While Corvette moved closer to the goal of being recognized as a true sports car, Thunderbird added features to make it more attractive to buyers seeking a "personal car." The most noticeable change was the addition of a rear mounted or "continental" spare tire. The removable hardtop took on optional "portholes" which, while tacky in appearance, may have helped relieve a blind spot. Functional vent doors were added to the front fenders to get cooler air in at the floor level. Over the course of the 1956 model year several engines were used. The base 292-cid, 202-horsepower V-8 was used only with manual transmission vehicles. The overdrive vehicles used a 312-cid engine producing 215 horsepower while the automatic version of that engine was rated at 225 horses. A late arrival was the 260 horsepower dual four-barrel option. The Thunderbird had cleaned up in the stock class in NASCAR Speedweeks, proving that it was very fast — in a straight line.

Clearly Ford saw a market for a small, high-styled car with excellent performance but the extreme rear positioning of that spare tire with its resulting effect on handling characteristics seems to confirm that they really weren't trying to pass the 1956 Thunderbird off as a sports car. At nearly 16,000 copies run off in 1956 it appears that Thunderbird had effectively tapped into the "personal car" market, whatever that was. Corvette, for its part, was doing well in the sports car market with almost 3,500 units. That's about five times the dismal 1955 total, and enough to guarantee that the Corvette would be back next year.

The real volume was in the full-size passenger

Mr. and Mrs. Duntov embrace at the peak after a successful record run.

cars and Chevrolet went all out there for 1956. The Ferrari-inspired grille had been slow to gain public acceptance in 1955 and Chevrolet quickly came up with an alternate to be used in the event that a mid-year change was necessary. Fortunately, the public soon warmed up to the '55 and sales took off. The proposed interim front-end design became part of the very successful facelift for the 1956 model year. The new grille extended the full width of the front end, incorporating rectangular parking lights in bright extensions that wrapped around the fenders to the wheel openings. The grille was slanted to give the impression that it was thrusting forward, and grille and hood were slightly v-eed for a prow shape. The overall appearance suggested speed.

In the rear, the taillight openings were enlarged with new bullet-shaped lenses incorporated in bright recessed housings. Taking a leaf from Cadillac's book, Chevrolet incorporated the fuel filler in the left taillight housing. In profile, the bumper ends continued the smooth flow of the quarter panel, another Cadillac feature. The quarter panels themselves were pulled back and down from the taillights for the illusion of greater length. This illusion was reinforced by the new Bel Air and 210-side trim that stretched from just behind the headlamp, curving down to the top of the rear bumper extension.

On the Bel Air, a second molding ran above and parallel to the first, reaching a point beyond the front door, then angled upward to the belt. On two-tone cars these moldings framed the paint break. The 210 level

vehicles were not treated to the upper molding, utilizing instead an angular sash molding that connected the body-side molding to the belt line at the point of the "dip." The 150 received bright windshield and backlight reveal moldings and a shorter version of the 210 body-side molding and sash. The 150 with its new trim took on a vastly improved exterior appearance. The municipal and taxi fleet buyers could probably have cared less about the improved appearance but the budget buyer was undoubtedly impressed.

An important new body style, the Sport Sedan, was introduced in the Bel Air and 210 series. This four-door hardtop body style was pioneered by Buick and Oldsmobile in 1955. The balance of the Bel Air line was carryover from 1955 with a familiar cast of characters: Sport Coupe, two-door sedan, four-door sedan, convertible, Beauville four-door station wagon (now rated for nine-passengers), and the Nomad two-door station wagon. The Nomad lost its unique full rear wheel openings and waffle pattern vinyl upholstery, now using the same smaller wheel opening and side trim as well as the upholstery treatment that characterized all Bel Airs.

On the subject of interiors, the 1956 Bel Air interiors were just right for their time. Convertibles were trimmed out in pattern vinyl (this vinyl had the appearance of cloth fabric with the weather-resistant qualities of vinyl) with bolsters in leather-grain vinyl trim. Other Bel Air models featured seating surfaces of pattern cloth with bolsters of leather-grain vinyl. The standard Bel Air interior color scheme was charcoal

Zora Arkus-Duntov blasts through a turn on his way up Pike's Peak in a 1956 Bel Air Sport Sedan. Note the skirts and wheelcovers installed earlier are now missing.

gray pattern cloth with ivory leather-grain vinyl. To avoid confusion here, it should be pointed out that, while this interior combination was merchandised as charcoal and ivory, most of us would probably see it as black and off-white. A number of very attractive two-tone custom-color interior combinations were available at extra cost. These interiors differed from the base in color only, using identical materials and sew patterns.

The Bel Air instrument panel trim for 1956 had a horizontal grid theme replacing the bow-tie pattern of 1955. The 210 interior was upgraded durability-wise with Starfrost leather-grain vinyl replacing the previous broadcloth trim on bolsters. A coarser pattern cloth than that used with the Bel Air was utilized for seating surfaces. As with the Bel Air, the standard combination was charcoal and ivory with custom-colored two-tone combinations available (and as with Bel Air, usually ordered). The 210 Station Wagons featured all-vinyl interiors for durability, and the Delray Club Coupe continued its traditional all-vinyl interior with unique biscuit sew pattern and fully carpeted floor. The custom-colored interiors were available on the Delray as well. The 210 series vehicles continued to feature front and rear armrests, dual sunvisors, cigarette lighter and horn ring.

The 150 series interior trims featured black pattern cloth seating surfaces with gold leather-grain vinyl bolsters. That "gold" was really a lot closer to cream. If the buyer wanted luxuries like front armrests and a cigarette lighter, there would be an extra charge.

Some, when writing about the 1956 Ford, have been critical of the lack of apparent change from the 1955 model. While it's true that it was a facelift, it was a good facelift. The appearance changes were mostly directed at making the 1955 Ford look more massive and more attractive for 1956. In that respect, the 1956 facelift should be considered a complete success. The weak link in Ford's 1956-product program actually seems to have been the way in which it was merchandised. While Chevrolet (and Plymouth) hammered away at racing and performance accomplishments, Ford's strategy was to stress safety features now available as standard or optional equipment. Things like the deep dish steering wheel that collapsed on impact to cushion the driver's chest and Lifeguard double grip door latches were standard on all Fords. Seatbelts, padded sunvisors and padded dash were options and Ford crafted its 1956 marketing theme on the benefits of these safety items.

Chevrolet, in a brilliant interception, worked safety into its performance ads and sent it right back at Ford with copy like "No other car has gone so high, so fast, so safely!" While promoting safety, Ford was still actively providing gratification to the go-fast crowd. The base engine continued to be the 137-horsepower I-Block 6, while the Y-Block V-8s started out with the 272 cid rated at 173 horsepower (176 with Ford-O-Matic). The Thunderbird 292 produced 200 horsepower (202 with Ford-O-Matic). A new 312-cid Thunderbird Special used with manual shift vehicles was good for 215 horses. That 312 cid, if used with Ford-O-Matic, got a four-barrel and pushed out 225 horsepower.

Two cars were used in the Pike's Peak hill climb. This one is the 1956 post four-door sedan.

Ford's restyling was especially effective on top-of-the-line Fairlane models which looked bigger and heavier thanks to large wraparound parking light units, wider, ribbed body side moldings, larger taillights and heavier deck lid trim in a "V" shape. The mid-level Customline took on a very clean look with revised side trim and, when equipped with extra cost fender skirts, was pretty close to sleek. The addition of windshield and backlight reveal moldings, along with a quarter panel molding, imparted a much-needed higher-price look to the base Mainline. When it came to interiors, the Ford was more or less comparable with the Mainline vs. the 150 and the Customline vs. the 210. When the Fairlane was stacked up against the Bel Air, it fell short. The Fairlane instrument panel lacked the glitter of the Bel Air panel and the sedan's patterned fabrics were both busy and lifeless.

Plymouth was the first in this class to offer tailfins, which arrived as part of the 1956 facelift. While not as "tacked-on" as some tailfins ('57 Lincoln, Nash and Hudson come to mind), they lacked the smooth integral look of big brothers, Chrysler and De Soto. The facelift for 1956 was generally considered successful with a new grille center, wheelcovers, various ornaments and revised side trim treatment for Belvederes. Inside, the temperature and oil gauges were moved from their odd right side position of 1955 to the left side where they became warning lights. The far-left side of the dash hosted the console panel for the new pushbutton transmission controls. A bright instrument panel applique added some needed up-level appeal.

Interiors of the three series, Belvedere, Savoy and Plaza were fairly colorful and typical of the period. Trim levels were similar to comparable Chevrolet and Ford models. Like Ford and Chevrolet, Plymouth added a four-door hardtop. Unlike Ford and Chevrolet, Plymouth had to engineer a complex double-folding rear door window to make the window disappear completely into the door.

Plymouth's base engine was now one of the few L-heads on the American market. The base V-8 268.8-cid engine was now producing 180 horsepower. The 276.1-cid V-8 developed 187 horsepower. Mid-year, Plymouth introduced the Fury, a two-door hardtop with a new 303-cid, four-barrel engine turning out 240 horsepower. Plymouth partisans belatedly got the car they were hoping for in 1955. The Fury was a separate model combining high performance with luxury trim and sporty appearance. Chevrolet had the Corvette sports car, Ford had the Thunderbird personal car and, now, Plymouth had the Fury, a really big, fast car. Plymouth's ad line was "Hotter Than The Hot One." The horsepower race was clipping right along.

When the numbers were added up, there were no surprises. Chevrolet was again first in sales with a healthy lead over number two Ford. Plymouth, which had stumbled badly in 1954, was still behind Buick in 1956, holding on to the fourth place in sales.

NASCAR Officials are shown measuring the ports of the four-barrel manifold on the 1956 Bel Air Sport Sedan. Note the false grille installed in front of the factory grille.

NATIONAL ASSOCIATION for STOCK CAR AUTO RACING, Inc.
42 SOUTH PENINSULA DRIVE, DAYTONA BEACH, FLORIDA

★ TELEPHONES: { 8525 / 8526

NATIONAL STOCK CAR RACING COMMISSION

E. G. "CANNONBALL" BAKER, INDIANAPOLIS, IND.
    NATIONAL COMMISSIONER
BILL FRANCE, DAYTONA BEACH, FLA.
    CHAIRMAN
ED OTTO, SOUTH ORANGE, N. J.
    VICE PRESIDENT
PAT PURCELL, DAYTONA BEACH, FLA.
    EXECUTIVE MANAGER
LOUIS OSSINSKY, DAYTONA BEACH, FLA.
    VICE PRESIDENT AND GENERAL COUNSEL
DON O'REILLY, DAYTONA BEACH, FLA.
    DIRECTOR, NASCAR NEWS BUREAU

SEPTEMBER 14, 1955

MR. THOMAS H. KEATING
VICE PRESIDENT AND DIRECTOR
GENERAL MOTORS CORPORATION
CHEVROLET DIVISION
DETROIT 2, MICHIGAN

DEAR MR. KEATING:

PLEASE PLACE THIS LETTER IN YOUR FILES AS A PERMANENT AND NOTARIZED RECORD OF
THE TIMES MADE BY TWO OF YOUR 1956 PRE-PRODUCTION MODEL CHEVROLETS.

THE TWO RUNS WERE MADE FROM THE STARTING LINE TO THE SUMMIT OF THE PIKES PEAK
HILLCLIMB COURSE, ON SEPTEMBER 9, 1955. BOTH CARS WERE DRIVEN UP THE HILL BY
MR. ZORA ARKUS-DUNTOV.

THE FIRST RUN WAS MADE AT 7:17 A.M. THE TWELVE AND A HALF MILE DISTANCE WAS
COVERED IN SEVENTEEN MINUTES, TWENTY-FOUR AND FIVE ONE HUNDRETHS SECONDS, FOR
A NEW RECORD FOR AMERICAN STOCK SEDANS. FIFTY MINUTES AFTER THE START OF THE
FIRST RUN, MR. DUNTOV HAD RETURNED TO THE STARTING LINE AND CHANGED AUTOMOBILES.
HE THEN DROVE THE SECOND CAR UP THE HILL IN AN ELAPSED TIME OF SEVENTEEN MINUTES,
FORTY-ONE AND NINETY-ONE ONE HUNDRETHS SECONDS. AFTER THE RUNS, THE CARS WERE
INSPECTED AND FOUND TO CONFORM WITH THE 1956 CHEVROLET SPECIFICATIONS. THE RUNS
WERE SANCTIONED, SUPERVISED AND TIMED BY NASCAR, THE NATIONAL ASSOCIATION FOR
STOCK CAR AUTO RACING.

OFFICIAL TIMER WAS JOSEPH EPTON. THE STARTING SUPERVISOR WAS JAMES A. PURCELL
AND THE COMMUNICATIONS WERE MANAGED BY MR. CECIL WOOD AND E. O. NAPELL. THE
RUNS WERE WITNESSED BY E.G. "CANNON BALL" BAKER, NATIONAL COMMISSIONER FOR STOCK
CAR RACING, AND FORMER HOLDER OF THE PIKES PEAK HILLCLIMB RECORD, AND WILLIAM
H. G. FRANCE, PRESIDENT OF NASCAR.

CONGRATULATIONS FOR A NEW PERFORMANCE RECORD FOR AMERICAN-BUILT FIVE PASSENGER
SEDANS.

VERY TRULY YOURS,

Bill France

BILL FRANCE

BF/JP

Dorothy W. Beech
Notary Public, State of Florida tt large
My commission expires July 28, 1959.
Bonded by American Surety Co. of N. Y.

This notarized letter from Bill France of NASCAR describes the Pike's Peak hill climb activity.

The Joie Chitwood Thrill Show had switched from Ford to Chevrolet. The 1956 Chevrolets shown here are actually retouched 1955 models.

The 1956 Corvette is posed with the new, more angular convertible top up.

Now in its second year, the 265 V-8 is displayed with all its attendant components.

The beautiful all-vinyl interior of the 1956 210 Club Coupe featured real carpet on the front and rear floors.

The testing device on the back bumper of this 1956 210 four-door sedan is known as a fifth wheel. It supplies data to on-board electric instruments.

We don't often see an ugly Corvette but this incomplete 1956 clay model comes pretty close.

The well trimmed door panel of a 1956 Bel Air Sport Sedan is displayed. This vehicle has power windows. Note the integral armrest.

A 1956 210 splashes through the water trough at GM's Milford, Michigan Proving Ground.

The 1956 Bel Air 210 four-door sedan looked very good when wearing a two-tone paint job.

The patterned cloth and vinyl interior of the 1956 210 was a big step down from that of a Bel Air.

Bel Air convertibles of any year were great looking cars and this 1956 is no exception.

This is the cheerful interior of a 1956 Bel Air Sport Coupe. Silver Mylar piping was an up-level feature at that time.

A magician is levitating a young lady to demonstrate the pillarless feature of the Bel Air Sport Sedan.

The new pointed grille, bumper and hood gave a slight prow-like effect to the front of the 1956 Bel Air Sport Coupe.

The new sweeping side trim of the 1956 Bel Air Sport Coupe resulted in a more flowing profile.

When seen at a low angle, 1956 Chevrolets like this Sport Sedan appeared to be taking off.

The advertising guys tried just about every stunt to call attention to the four-door pillarless hardtop features of the Sport Sedan. Here we have identically dressed twins.

While the roofline did not flow quite as smoothly as that of the Sport Coupe, the 1956 Bel Air Sport Sedan was still a good-looking automobile.

This is the 1956 Bel Air four-door sedan. This model got very little advertising attention with the new Sport Sedan hogging the spotlight, but it remained the best-selling Bel Air by a wide margin.

The three-seat, nine-passenger Station Wagon returned in 1956. This is the Bel Air Beauville. This was one of the industry's best looking four-door wagons. Maybe the very best looking.

The two-door sedan was the third best seller in the Bel Air line in 1956, just behind the Sport Coupe.

The wraparound parking light housings, shown on a Bel Air Sport Coupe, lent a Cadillac-like air to the 1956 Chevrolet.

'56

The 1956 150 series received a nice appearance upgrade with the body side trim and bright windshield and backlight moldings.

Sporting two-tone paint and the new standard molding package, even the lowest cost 1956 Chevrolet wagon, this 150 two-door Handyman, was an attractive vehicle.

Chevrolet's new
concept car for
the 1956 show
season was the
Impala, a large
two-door
Hardtop with a
number of
Corvette styling
cues.

A 1956 Bel Air Convertible has pulled up to the pumps of a typical Sunoco station for service.

The attendant is showing the driver of the 1956 Bel Air Convertible a new T-3 sealed beam headlamp. Note the accessory spotlight.

The 50,000,000th GM car, a 1955 Bel Air, was built in November of 1954. This car was the 35,000,000th Chevrolet. It was built in May of 1956. The flags identify the years of other Chevrolet milestones.

A 1956 Bel Air Sport Coupe is joining a 150 sedan on a carrier pulled by a cab-over-engine Chevrolet tractor.

The side trim on the 1956 150 Sedan Delivery lacked the vertical sash molding used on the Handyman wagon.

This guy looks a little big for the cockpit of a 1956 Corvette, but nobody wanted to tell him he couldn't drive it.

This radio display was developed as a point-of-purchase aid in Chevrolet showrooms to help sell radios with new 1956 Chevrolets.

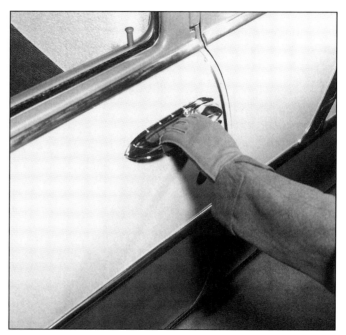

Accessory door handle guards prevented paint scratches behind and immediately around the door handles and added some sparkle as well.

The model is demonstrating the accessory day/night mirror installed in a 1956 210.

Fender ornaments, styled to match the hood ornament, were extra cost dealer-installed accessories in 1956.

The compass and tissue dispenser shown on this 1956 210 are sought after items among today's restorers.

The recessed location of the 1956 fuel filler didn't leave a lot of space for maneuvering the key for a locking gas cap.

The accessory seat belts of 1956 were wide and employed a massive buckle.

The model is
demonstrating the
release mechanism
for the Chevrolet
authorized rear
mounted tire.

The attractive profile of this 1956 Nomad is marred by the dirty looking whitewalls. Actually they aren't dirty, they are still wearing the blue protective coating characteristic of factory fresh tires.

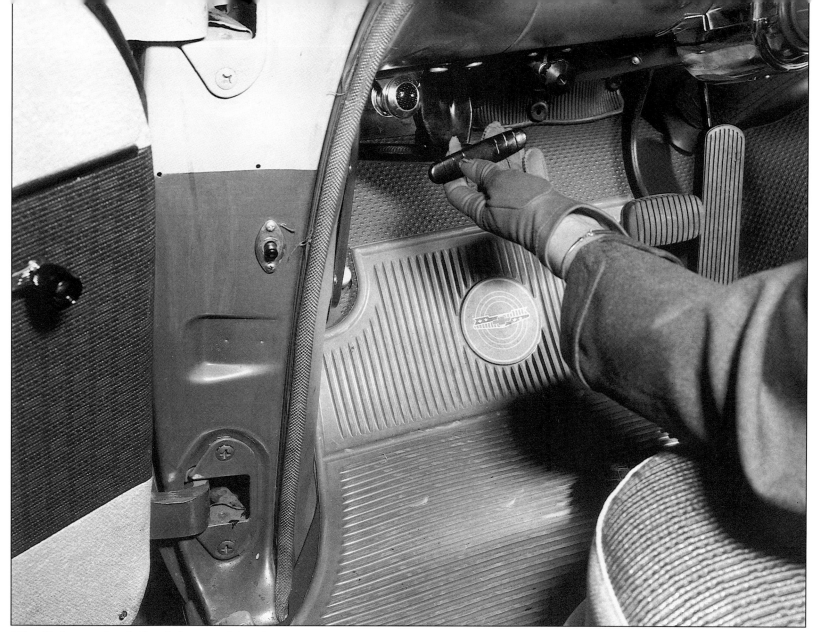

The light to the left of the parking brake is an accessory warning light to remind drivers to release the brake before starting out. Note the correct 1956 accessory floor mat. And, there's no serial number plate on the cowl post.

Like in the sales race, a 1956 Chevrolet leads a pair of 1956 Fords in a stock car event, possibly at the North Wilkesboro Speedway.

This shot portrays the good life in 1956. A new V-8 Nomad and a contemporary house. What more could one want?

The new quarter panels for 1956 are shown to good advantage at this angle on a Nomad.

At this low 3/4-front angle, a parked 1956 Bel Air Sport Coupe appears to be leaping ahead.

The sleek new lines of the 1956 Corvette are complimented by the new removable fiberglass hardtop.

A new 1956 Bel Air four-door sedan has arrived in the service department of Wink Chevrolet in Detroit, most likely for a routine check-up.

A dealer sponsored stock car, number 32, was displayed on the showroom floor of Detroit's Wink Chevrolet in June 1956.

When seen directly from the rear, a two-tone 1956 Bel Air, like this convertible, could appear to be a single color while it would be yet a different color if viewed directly from the front.

This two-tone V-8 210 Townsman has no other visible options. It is a six-passenger four-door station wagon.

The 1956 210 Sport Coupe provided the sleek, pillarless styling of a two-door hardtop at a cost of less then $40 above a Bel Air two-door sedan.

The fact that this 1956 Chevrolet 210 two-door station wagon was powered by a V-8 was evidenced by the "V" on the hood.

This 1956 210 Del Ray Club Coupe had an accessory continental tire and the very attractive wire covers that were installed over the base hubcaps.

A "loaded" 1956 Bel Air four-door sedan shows off the accessory fender guards, fender top ornaments, rear antenna, sill molding, wire covers and more.

This 1956 150 four-door sedan is ready for the rigors of taxi duty with a heavy-duty grille guard, spot-light and no-nonsense mirror.

The optional padded dash shown on a 1956 Bel Air was both functional and attractive.

This 1956 Bel Air Sport Sedan was equipped with a V-8 with radio, two-tone paint and whitewalls. The position of the shift lever, seen through the windshield, indicates that it also had Powerglide.

Parked in front of Detroit's Cody High School, this 1956 Bel Air four-door sedan is wearing a sample driver's education sign. Any Chevrolet merchandising material that is marked "home town" or "your town" or "any town" is a sample used for solicitation purposes.

Chevrolet's lowest-priced 1956 car was this perky 150 three-passenger Utility Sedan. This vehicle replaced the previous business coupe. It dedicated the rear compartment to a platform for carrying sample cases or other cargo. The only visible options are the whitewall tires.

(Left)
A marshaling yard at the Flint, Mich. assembly plant had this mouth-watering selection of newly-assembled 1956 Chevrolets, including at least 28 Bel Air convertibles.

It's a two-door on one side, a four-door on the other. This clay model shot in August of 1954, depicts a proposal for 1956. Note the small 1955 "V" emblems have been moved from under the taillight to under the headlight.

In 1956 an independent Detroit firm, Allender, modified Chevrolet convertibles and hardtops to "El Moroccos." Just how closely they resembled the then-current Cadillac Eldorado was illustrated in this shot, which captured a real 1956 Cadillac Eldorado (left) and a 1956 El Morocco (right) parked on a Detroit street.

Stock car racing of 1956 involved actual stock cars like this Bel Air running in the convertible class. In those days the "little guys" would reinstall the lights, wheelcovers and exhaust system after the race and drive to the next event. Primitive perhaps, but more fun. Note the elevated flagman.

The famous factory sponsored Thunderbird of Chuck Daigh awaits its turn to run on the sand at Daytona in 1956, where he posted a winning speed of 88.779 mph for the stock sports car class in the measured mile. While he set records for acceleration with his supercharged 'Bird, he never got a shot at the Flying Mile top end run as he was disqualified when his car failed to make the starting grid in time.

Just about everything ran at Daytona Speedweek in 1956, including this 1956 Chevrolet patrol car belonging to some unknown sheriff's department.

The new Sport Sedan was available in Bel Air or 210 trim in 1956. This is the seldom seen 210 version, which was outsold by the Bel Air at a ratio of about five-to-one.

This young lady has elected to park under a lonely freeway interchange and lean on her totally base 150 four-door sedan.

In its second year in the Corvette, the 265 V-8 was available with this dual quad set-up.

This two-tone 210 four-door Townsman Station Wagon had a V-8 engine and no other options. It was available only in six-passenger configuration.

Two-tone paint, whitewalls and V-8 engine are the only extra cost items showing on this 1956 210 Del Ray Club Coupe, which is externally identical to the 210 two-door sedan.

All 1956 Bel Air four-door Beauville Station Wagons were nine-passenger models. This one is a two-tone V-8 with whitewalls.

Take a 1956 210 four-door, add all this glittery stuff and you'll have a very expensive 210. Accessories include exhaust extension, continental tire, fender guards, license plate frame, wire wheel trim, sill moldings and more.

It was Chevrolet's practice to load a car with accessories (sometimes referred to a "spot car") and send it out to auto shows. This 1956 210 four-door is one of those cars. It is a six-cylinder with fender ornaments, fender guards, wire wheel trim, mirror, sill moldings and more.

An early pre-production 1956 Bel Air Sport Coupe was shot in the design check area at the Chevrolet Engineering Center, in Warren, Mich., where the car was developed.

In November of 1955, a 1956 Ford Fairlane, a 1956 Plymouth Belvedere and a 1956 Chevrolet 210, all two-door hardtops, posed for this portrait in the styling courtyard at the GM Technical Center. The 1956 Plymouth and Chevrolet both featured visored headlamps, but Plymouth's were set lower and were more deeply tunneled. Those Plymouth grilles live on in today's lead sled customs.

This 1956 Corvette was customized for Prince Bertil of Sweden. Modifications included grille, wire wheels, narrow whitewalls, a "V" replacing the front header emblem and a quarter panel exhaust outlet. This vehicle uses late style production chrome headlamp bezels.

This 1956 Bel Air Station Wagon was upgraded at styling with a carpeted cargo floor and bright skid strips. It was probably done for an executive or celebrity.

A mix of 1956-57 vehicles on display in the styling dome in November 1955. Included are (front row): a 1956 Nash, 1956 Ford, 1956 Chevrolet, 1957 Chevrolet and 1956 Plymouth. The Buicks on the raised stage are 1956 and 1957 models.

This 1956 Bel Air Convertible was modified (we called it de-chroming at the time) at styling for an executive's wife. Check the excellent fit of the convertible top.

Here's a clay model proposal for a 1956 Bel Air two-door sedan. The front bumper treatment looks a bit like the one that wound up on the 1957 Buick.

MADLER
11-30-54

9651

This early prototype 1956 Bel Air four-door sedan shows a proposed exhaust port in the right bumper end.

This is a staged shot on a banked track showing a 1956 150 modified for a NASCAR sanctioned 24-hour record setting event at Darlington. The event was code named "operation carousel" because the car went round and round. Although this shot is intended to convey speed the speedometer reads "0".

This shot clearly shows how the wire wheel trim was installed over the base 1956 Chevrolet hubcap. Those wide clips were fitted to the edge of the wheel and folded-in. Olds used a similar system in the 1960s.

This 1956 auto show shot shows a wall poster featuring the Bel Air Sport Sedan running up Pike's Peak. The 210 Beauville is wearing the accessory grille and fender guards. The Bel Air has a plastic insert in the door to reveal the new door latch with safety interlock. It's an interesting contrast of appeals to performance and safety.

This brand new 1956 Bel Air Convertible is wearing whitewalls with no other options visible. From the lowest-cost 150 to the best Bel Air, you needed only to add whitewalls to any 1956 Chevrolet to have a great looking car.

57

It's Speedweeks at Daytona Beach in 1957 and this new Bel Air Sport Sedan is kicking up the sand as it fires off the starting line.

1957:
Hood rockets and tail fins!

Chevrolet entered 1957 with the confidence that comes from knowing you have a good product. General Motors was operating on a three-year life cycle for major model changes, and since Cadillac, Buick and Oldsmobile had been all new in 1954, they would be completely new for 1957. Chevrolet and Pontiac would go into the third year of their 1955 bodies in 1957 and would be all new in 1958. Conventional wisdom held that this would be safe because Chrysler Corporation (it appeared at that point in the program) would be riding with facelifts of its 1955 bodies, although Ford and Mercury would be all new. In 1957 Chevrolet's image leader, the Corvette, caught fire. The Powerglide and Blue Flame Six combination of 1953 and 1954 had not penetrated the sports car market, the same car with a 265 V-8 didn't get the job done in 1955 either. The restyle and refinement program of 1956 finally turned the Corvette around in the marketplace. But, it was in 1957 that a number of product improvements converged to produce a sports car that couldn't be ignored. At the start of the model year, the new 283-cid V-8 replaced the previous 265 cid. In base form with four-barrel carb, the horsepower rating was 220 (RPO 469) with two four-barrels and hydraulic lifters was rated at 245 horsepower. If RPO 469 was specified with mechanical lifters and a high-lift cam, the horsepower jumped to 270. There were also two new fuel-injected versions. RPO 579 with hydraulic lifters turned out 250 horsepower. By selecting mechanical lifters and a high-lift cam with RPO 579, the amazing figure of 283 horses, one-per-cubic inch, was attained. On April 9, 1957, Corvettes started to receive four-speed manual transmissions. By year's end, 10.5 percent of 1957 Corvettes had been so equipped. The 1956 Corvette had been an uncommonly good-looking car and, wisely, the appearance was virtually unaltered for 1957. The base of the rearview mirror was modified to eliminate the knurled head adjustment screw that characterized the 1956 models. Of course, the emblems added to the sides and trunk of fuel-injected Corvettes would also provide model year identification. Additionally, many unseen or hidden modifications occurred including aluminum channel reinforcements in doors as well as underbody and dash reinforcements.

Clearly, the Corvette was now in a position to get the attention and respect that Chevrolet had wanted all along. It was, perhaps, summed up best in Trend

This display was in the lobby of the GM Building in Detroit at announcement time. No, those aren't ghosts; the transparent nature of the people is the result of a very slow shutter speed.

Books' *1957 Cars of the World.* "The Corvette is the closest automobile to the purist's definition of a sports car that is manufactured in any quantity in America today." The public seemed equally impressed, buying almost twice as many 1957 Corvettes.

Over in the personal car market segment, Thunderbird was sailing right along in its last year as a two-passenger car. The difference in approach of these vehicles is seen when quoting again from *1957 Cars of the World:* "Performance-wise, Thunderbirds are plenty hot when it comes to acceleration, but road-ability is not considered to be on par with some of the European sports cars." In base trim the Thunderbird boasted a 292-cid Y-Block V-8 developing 212 horsepower. The first option was a 312 cid rated at 245 horsepower. When the 312 sported dual quads the rating jumped to 270. A hotter version developed 285 horses. Not enough? How about 312 horsepower with a Paxton-McCulloch supercharger? Just a handful more than 200 of these "F-Birds" were built in 1957.

Although the T-Bird would abandon the two-passenger concept the following year, it was nevertheless, extensively facelifted for 1957. Extended rear quarter panels incorporated low, flared fins. The new front bumper and grille ensemble gave a massive, open-mouth look to what would be the best looking and best selling of the "little Birds."

The 1957 Chevrolet must be one of the most famous production cars in the world. It is hard to think of another single model that is used more often in advertising or TV commercials. It is the icon of the 1950s.

Continuing past practice, the series lineup was again 150, 210 and Bel Air. While sharing much with its 1956 predecessor, the 1957 Chevrolet had many modifications, big and little. The cowl, for example, was lowered 1.5 inches in a series of changes that eliminated the previous air intake that ran across the cowl ahead of the windshield. Fresh air was now brought in through screens incorporated in the upper portion of the headlamp bezels. This fresh air was carried back to the passenger compartment through ducts in the top of each front fender. All front sheet metal, as well as the bumper and grille, was completely new. Where the 1956 had taken on a prow shape, the 1957 front-end theme reverted to the blunt, flat look of the 1955.

The new full-width grille and bumper ensemble, while separate, worked together as a single styling element. The grille, a horizontal mesh unit of stamped aluminum, was recessed. On Bel Air models an anodized gold grille was substituted for the normal silver tone of the 150 and 210 models. A floating grille bar incorporated the Chevrolet emblem in the center and the parking lights at each end. The hood was carried low between the high front fenders and was adorned by twin recessed windsplits, or hood ornaments, if you prefer. Thin blisters flowed back from the windsplits, adding torsional strength to the large, flat panel. A "Chevrolet" script was centered on the hood's front surface. If the vehicle was equipped

The attractive and spacious 150 Sedan Delivery is seen in the prep area of a Detroit Chevrolet dealership.

with a V-8 engine, a broad chrome V underlined the script. If the vehicle was a Bel Air, a gold V was used in place of chrome.

Just to the rear of the headlight, each front fender carried a series of three vertical indentations. Bel Airs were again singled out for special treatment with these indentations filled with gold hashmarks. Chevrolet referred to these as "gold-anodized aluminum fender louvers." Moving around to the side, the doors, windshield and roof were similar in appearance to those of 1955 and 1956. The rear quarter panels were raised and pulled back several inches, forming low, tasteful fins. While some fins rose dramatically to tower over the decklid, Chevrolet's fins were hardly noticeable from a 3/4-front view. In a low 3/4-rear view they took on a more dominant look, raking back and away from the flat decklid. The effect was most pronounced on the Nomad with its forward slanted tailgate. On Nomads the inside portion of the extended fin formed a large triangle when viewed from the side. In years to come Chevrolet's fins were fondly remembered while some others (like '59 Cadillac, '61 Imperial, '60 Plymouth) became examples of styling excess. The 1957 Chevrolet catalog, by the way, called these "high-set rear fenders."

Moving to the rear the appearance was definitely new. Flat, deeply contoured bumpers were finished off at each end by protruding pods which simulated exhaust ports. The catalog refers to these as bumper guards. The lower portion of the "guard" had a knockout provision for the installation of optional backup lights. Directly above these "guards" the

cathedral shape tail light lenses were housed in chrome bezels from which fender end moldings rose up and over the quarter panels. A swing-away panel in the left molding concealed the fuel filler. The broad, flat deck lid no longer had an emblem. A simple "Chevrolet" script was used, underlined by a broad V on V-8 vehicles. Again, as on the hood, the V was gold if used on a Bel Air.

The side trim differed from series to series with 150 models receiving a simple quarter panel molding treatment consisting of a single horizontal molding connected by a sash molding to the belt at the body "dip" point. On 210 models a molding extended from a point near the bottom of the headlight, sweeping down to meet the bumper at the trailing edge of the quarter panel. On the rear door of four-door models, or the quarter panel of two-door models, a second molding rose up and back to run parallel to the top of the quarter panel. This formed the color break for two-tone vehicles.

Bel Air models used the 210 moldings and added some more bright work of their own. Most noticeable was the quarter panel area in which the 210 color break was filled with a ribbed anodized aluminum insert set off with a Chevrolet emblem and gold "Bel Air" script. The quarter panel peak molding was longer, extending to a point above the centerline of the rear wheel. On sedans and four-door wagons, additional bright moldings were added to the upper doors and the windshield posts for more high-level glitter.

Chevrolet's most popular station wagon, a 210 four-door Townsman, has been outfitted with a tent for carefree camping.

The original plan called for a different exterior trim treatment. The 210 models were not supposed to get the upper molding that created the paint break. The plan called for only the molding that extended the entire length of the vehicle. Two-tones would be created by applying a contrasting color from the belt down to that molding. That plan was revised only at, or past, the eleventh hour, after incorrect shots were distributed in press kits and the first catalog printing was released with incorrect art. The first catalogs also illustrated a Bel Air Townsman wagon without the anodized quarter panel inserts, illustrating instead, the two-tone insert that wound up on the 210. In the first edition catalog, the "ribbed two-tone silver anodized aluminum panel on rear fender" was listed as optional at extra cost. Perhaps the standard anodized aluminum treatments on Ford's Custom 300 and Fairlane 500 prompted the late upgrade on the 210 and Bel Air.

Interior trims were once again modified for 1957. In keeping with its status on the price ladder, the 150 interior was simple. In keeping with the times, the silver and black interior with random pattern black on gray cloth seat and door panel inserts looked very much like a mid-1950s kitchen set. The 210 series offered several two-tone color combinations to harmonize with the wide variety of exterior combinations. The historic upgrades over the 150, armrests, horn ring, right sunvisor, color-keyed floor covering and upgraded upholstery, were continued. The Delray Club Coupe made one last appearance in 1957 as a special model in the 210 series. It again featured an all vinyl interior but lacked the unique and highly attractive biscuit sew pattern of previous years.

The Bel Air continued to carry the luxury torch, and did it very well. Colorful vinyl seat bolsters framed Jacquard-loomed cloth highlighted with color-keyed nylon flecks on pillared sedans. Hardtops substituted a random pattern Jacquard cloth for the flecked cloth of the sedans. Convertible and Nomad trims were all vinyl. Door panels were trimmed with matching vinyl accented with bright moldings. Separate armrests returned this year, replacing the integral units found on the doors of 1955 and 1956 Bel Air models. Floor carpeting was, of course, standard.

The new instrument panel was no longer symmetrical. The speedometer and all instruments were housed in circular pods incorporated as a unit under a raised ledge in the otherwise low instrument panel, referred to by Chevrolet as the "flight" panel. A recessed cove housing all control knobs, the standard clock and the optional radio, ran the width of the panel. The cove was trimmed with a bright, textured applique.

Every so often an idea will sweep the auto industry and many makes will introduce the same feature in the same year. So it was with the large-scale jump from 15" to 14" tires in 1957. It was an easy way to lower the car without making serious body or chassis modifications.

In a year of otherwise safe and prudent engineering, Chevrolet introduced the Turboglide. In

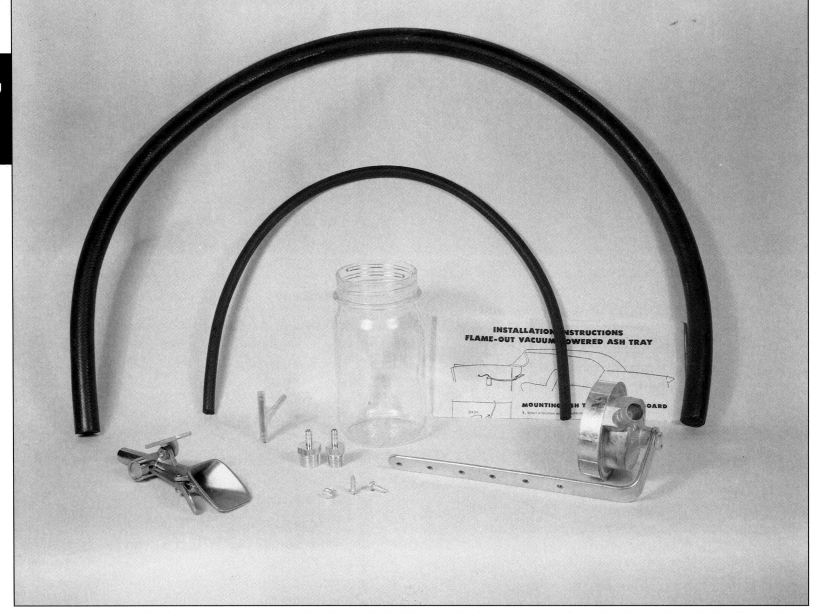

You've never heard of a vacuum-powered ashtray? Well, here is the one merchandised for the 1957 Chevrolet. It mounted under the dash and dumped into a bottle mounted in the engine bay.

use, the Turboglide would be more familiar than Powerglide to drivers of modern vehicles. Whereas Powerglide placed Reverse at the right end of the selector quadrant, Turboglide positioned reverse in the now familiar position between Park and Neutral. However, rather than Low, Turboglide used the terminology "Hill Retarder." The catalog explained it as follows: "To help save your car's brakes, Hill Retarder gives extra braking on steep downgrades." On paper it looked like a winner. As the catalog said: "Chevrolet pioneers again introducing still another engineering first! This all-new automatic drive puts three turbines to work, bringing new smoothness and performance to the low-price field! With an infinitely variable torque ratio from standstill to cruising speed, you experience an unbroken flow of power and not the slightest hint of a shift. Single forward drive range. Amazing new Hill Retarder. All this is achieved with less weight, fewer parts and simpler controls!"

The Turboglide with die-cast aluminum housing weighed much less than the Powerglide, and in fact, was only four pounds heavier than the manual transmission. Turboglide was smooth — shifts were not felt, and had good torque multiplication characteristics, but it was not known for durability. By 1960, Chevrolets with Turboglide were a hard sell on used car lots.

The base engine continued to be the familiar 235-cid Blue Flame Six rated at 140 horsepower and available with three-speed, overdrive or Powerglide. The Turbofire 265-cid, two-barrel, 162-horse V-8 made one last appearance in three-speed or overdrive cars only. The Turbofire 283-cid, two-barrel, 185-horse V-8 was available with Powerglide or Turboglide only. The Super Turbofire four-barrel V-8 was rated at 220 horsepower and was available in combination with any transmission. Moving to two four-barrels resulted in a rating of 245-horses with hydraulic lifters. When the 245-horse engine was specified any transmission was available, including a close-ratio three-speed. If Powerglide was ordered, a heavy-duty Corvette unit was supplied. The dual-quad 283 V-8 was also available with solid lifters and was rated at 270 horsepower in that configuration. The close-ratio three-speed was the only transmission available with that option.

Two fuel-injection options were offered. The fuel-injected 283 V-8 turned out 250 horsepower when equipped with hydraulic lifters and could be combined with three-speed, close-ratio three-speed, Turboglide, or the heavy-duty Powerglide. The all-out performance favorite was the fuel-injected 283 V-8 with solid lifters which kicked out 283 horsepower — one horsepower per cubic inch. This powerhouse was available only with the close-ratio three-speed. Just think about it: in 1951 the biggest engine in a U.S. passenger car was the 180 horsepower Chrysler Firepower. Only six years later, Chevrolet's lowest power V-8 automatic transmission combination developed 185 horsepower and ran circles around that heavy old Chrysler. Yes, the horsepower race had come to John Q. Citizen and he was enjoying it.

Reliable Chevrolet company was typical of a modern small town dealership in 1957. It actually looks like three pole barns shoved together with an add-on showroom.

Then there was Ford. Or perhaps it would be more appropriate to say "then there were Fords." Yes, there were two Fords in 1957. There were the Custom and Custom 300 on a 116-inch wheelbase. All wagons used the 116-inch platform. Fairlane and Fairlane 500 models were 207.7 inches overall. That was 7.7 inches longer than Chevrolet. The Custom and Custom 300 were rather conservative in design while the Fairlane and Fairlane 500 were somewhat more high style. All hardtops were in the longer series. Because there were two series, each with two trim levels, it was somewhat difficult to make a direct comparison of the Fairlane and Fairlane 500 models to Chevrolet. The Customs were pretty close to the 150 and the Custom 300 was comparable to the 210. The Fairlane and Fairlane 500 were generally priced to straddle the Bel Air. For the last few years, Buick's Special had been harvesting many buyers from the upper part of the low-price field. Buick, in fact, had displaced Plymouth in the third place slot in 1954. Now Ford would make a run on the bottom of the middle-price field with the Fairlane 500. Later in the year, the Fairlane formed the basis for the Edsel Ranger and Pacer models in the middle price field.

Ford really couldn't compete with the unique design of the Nomad wagon but they had a unique model of their own in the new Skyliner. The Skyliner was a convertible whose all-steel hardtop rose, slid back, and nested in the rear deck. Well, it did all that if everything was working all right. Sometimes it just rose and stayed there. The roof was shorter than that of a conventional Victoria and the deck was longer and higher. While some loved it, there were those who thought the profile was too close to that of the then common flower cars used in funeral processions. And it was expensive. Luggage space, being confined to a small (6.5 cubic foot) box in the center of that seemingly huge trunk area, was all but non-existent as well.

Ford's base engine was the 223-cid 6-cylinder, now rated at 144 horsepower. The base V-8, the 272 cid, developed 190 horsepower. The four-barrel Thunderbird V-8, displacing 292 cid, was rated at 212 horsepower. The Thunderbird Special continued to feature 312 cid. In single four-barrel form it developed 245 horsepower. Two dual-quad versions were rated at 270 and 285 horses. Two Supercharged Thunderbird Specials (code E) were cataloged at 300 and 340 horsepower but there is some question as to whether any of the 340-horse versions were actually sold.

This was definitely Plymouth's year to shine with a new, modern chassis featuring torsion bar front suspension, an efficient three-speed automatic transmission and styling that was very right for the time. True, that styling was too radical for some, but Plymouth's stodgy reputation had not been completely erased by the more contemporary 1955 and 1956 models. Some dramatic action was necessary to get the image that Plymouth needed. Plymouth had come a long way from the frumpy days of 1954 and had, in fact, made a giant leap in just one model year to get to that 1957 model. In that light it is not surprising that

This styling model from 1955 showed a 150 four-door sedan with the type of skirts that showed up on the 1957 Mercury Turnpike Cruiser. It also boasts twin rear antennas and anodized deck lid trim.

Plymouth's 1957 ad line was "Suddenly its 1960." Plymouth's Plaza, Savoy and Belvedere were positioned to compete against Chevrolet's 150, 210 and Bel Air. Across the board, they were almost always within $20 of one another. The Fury two-door hardtop Coupe continued as a separate model with unique appearance and performance features coupled with special up-level interior trim. Several 1957 Furys have been restored as convertibles and eventually somebody is bound to create documentation to legitimize one of these as a "rare factory special." Be skeptical.

In 1960 Plymouth would swing over to the famed "Slant Six;" for 1957 however, the base engine continued to be the venerable 230-cid Flathead 6 developing 132 horsepower. The base V-8, a 276-cid unit, was rated at 197 horsepower. It was used in Plaza models only. The base Savoy and Belvedere V-8 displaced 299 cid and produced 215 horsepower. A four-barrel version raised horsepower to 235. The base Fury used the 299 with four-barrel. A Fury option was the 318-cid V-8 with two-four barrel carbs rated at 290 horsepower.

Although the horsepower race didn't get off the ground in the low-price field until 1955, by 1957 the buyers actually had more power available than most of them were willing to buy. For the most part, dual quads, superchargers and fuel injection were considered overkill. The kids were lucky if Dad bought a V-8 with four-barrel and most were forced to content themselves with a base two-barrel V-8. If it was a 283 Chevy, the kid could still have a lot of fun.

It now seems unlikely that such a likable and durable car as the 1957 Chevrolet suffered so much in the marketplace. In the end Ford scored a decisive victory over Chevrolet to regain first place for the first time since 1935. And it wasn't a cliffhanger. Ford ran up a sizable lead in the range of 140,000 vehicles, 25 percent of the total market. Chevrolet pulled 24.3 percent of the market. Plymouth was the spoiler with an even 10 percent of the market which was good enough for third place. The tremendous appeal of that car probably contributed to Chevrolet's poor sales. The last laugh would be Chevrolet's as many of the 1957 Fords and Plymouths were so bad that they became excellent testimonials for Chevrolet.

This 1957 Bel Air Sport Coupe is an early prototype. The steering wheel is of 1956 design and that front wheel cover is very crude. While it has a continental kit, it is missing several moldings and the hood wind splits.

This is Ford's new 1957 Skyliner retractable hardtop. The short roof and high deck gave it the profile of a funeral flower car.

This 1957 Bel Air Sport Sedan was flagged into Los Angeles on announcement day late in 1956. The car had an emergency light on the package shelf, a two-way radio and Michigan plates. A flagman is in attendance with a group of greeters. It was apparently a timed run from some point to L.A. but the exact purpose is no longer known.

The author had a 210 Handyman wagon like this one in about 1965. It was a V-8 overdrive in two-tone blue. He would like to buy it again for the same price: $85.

A two-tone 1957 Bel Air V-8 two-door sedan with whitewalls pauses along California's Pacific Coast.

One of a series of show cars done by female designers in 1957, this Bel Air Convertible was named "Mademoiselle." Exterior differences are subtle; color key paint fill in wheelcovers and in quarter panel trim. The greatest effort was devoted to interior upgrades.

This is the interior of the Mademoiselle show car, a 1957 Chevrolet Bel Air Convertible. The multi-color inserts predicted the 1958 and 1959 Impala interiors. It appears that this seat was placed in the car but not centered and bolted down. That would explain the unusual expanse of floor beyond the sill plate.

This 1957 Chevrolet Bel Air Sport Coupe show car was one of a series done by GM's women designers. Note the color-keyed fill on the wheelcovers and the white interior.

MADLER
10-25-56

14740

Sleek but trouble prone is a good way to describe this 1957 Plymouth Belvedere. Compare the huge door gaps with the tight gaps on Chevrolets in this section. Those dramatic front fender "eyebrows" rusted badly.

This was "show and tell" day in September 1956 at Styling and the employees drove their own personal 'Vettes to be parked in the styling patio with several show cars. Second from right is Chuck Jordan, who would go on to become vice president of styling for GM.

The cargo deck of a 1957 210 Townsman wagon was done in ribbed linoleum. The lower tailgate was supported by cables.

A 1957 Chevrolet 210 Townsman four-door station wagon poses outside the Styling Dome at the GM Technical Center. This vehicle is a six-passenger with whitewalls and an outside mirror.

The patterned cloth and ribbed vinyl identifies this as a 1957 Bel Air interior. Note that the armrest is no longer integral with the door panel.

The lively rear compartment of a 1957 Bel Air four-door sedan was a complex mixture of cloth and several types of vinyl.

MADLER
3-29-57

15897

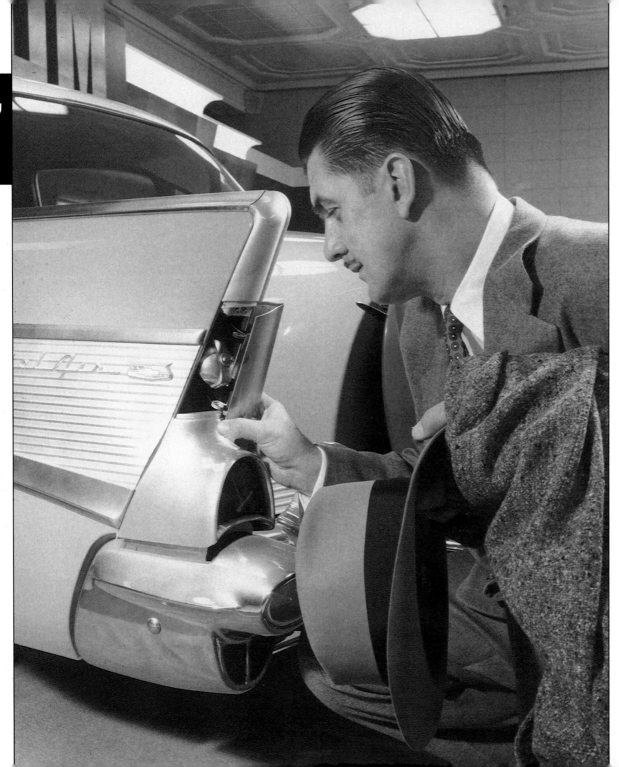

This gentleman is showing us how to access the fuel filler on the new 1957 Chevrolets. The Bel Air shown has extra cost back-up lights.

This 1957 Nomad is a V-8 with whitewalls. Although lacking the unique rear wheel opening of the 1955 Nomad, the 1957 side trim complemented the Nomad very successfully.

The 1957 Bel Air Sport Sedan shown here has the knockout plates in the bumper pods where the back-up lights would be installed.

A 1957 Bel Air Sport Coupe seems to be driving out of the Pacific Ocean. In the very near future, things with funny names like Toyota and Datsun would rise from that same ocean to bedevil Chevrolet and the rest of the domestic industry.

A late prototype build 1957 Bel Air is seen in profile. The top fit is a bit loose on this one.

A prototype 1957 210 Sport Sedan shows the originally planned molding treatment.

An excellent but seldom seen angle which makes the 1957 Bel Air Convertible look even longer and lower than it really is.

This dramatic angle shows a 1957 Bel Air V-8 with extra cost bumper guards and back-up lights. To facilitate lifting the decklid, finger grips were provided in the "V".

This well dressed 1957 Bel Air has backup lights, bumper guards and an incorrect for 1957 license plate frame. Note the plate reads "1-USA" not the more familiar "USA-1".

This 1957 Bel Air is a six-passenger Townsman four-door station wagon with whitewalls and two-tone paint.

A close look at the instrument panel of this 1957 Bel Air reveals that it is not equipped with a radio, although it has several exterior options.

The marshaling yard at the Flint assembly plant was the location of this line of 210s and Bel Airs.

The flying salt spray was a necessary evil if you planned to run your new 1957 Bel Air during Speedweeks at Daytona Beach.

Maybe, if the author had been driving a fuel-injected Bel Air in 1957 instead of a 1952 Nash, he would have met this young lady. Or maybe not.

Number 441, a fuel-injected 1957 150 Business Sedan, appears to have been brand new when this shot was taken in Daytona in February, 1957.

This 1957 150 four-door sedan was a six-cylinder built to U.S. Air Force specifications.

Chevrolet's lowest price four-door station wagon in 1957 was in the 210 series, not the 150 series. So, instead of getting the usual bare-bones model, the U.S. Army received this more upscale 210 Townsman.

An almost sinister look is presented by this 1957 Corvette in black with blackwall tires. The Ray Whyte dealership was in Grosse Pointe, Michigan.

Wearing standard hubcaps and optional whitewalls, this 1957 210 Sport Coupe is a V-8 with no other visible options.

Here we have a Bel Air sedan front compartment. Note the "power brake" imprint on the brake pedal pad.

The 210 was Chevrolet's most popular two-door sedan. It is seen in V-8 form with two-tone paint and whitewalls. This is otherwise a base car.

A 1957 Ford Fairlane 500 and a 1957 Bel Air are posed together in the styling courtyard at the GM Technical Center. The Ford roof appears lower and flatter, but the Chevrolet headlight treatment is more impressive. Compare the position of the steering wheels.

The 1957 Bel Air Sport Sedan featured a broad band of stainless to highlight the side windows.

This late pre-production 1957 Bel Air Sport Coupe was posed in the Styling Dome. The front ride height seems to be slightly low in comparison to later production jobs.

A great fin shot which also gives a good look at the optional backup light lens.

It required the efforts of five strong young men to install the front bumper on a 1957 Chevrolet 210. The location was identified as the Van Nuys plant. If so, it suggests that some California cars did not get the famous one-piece bumper.

Chevrolet's best seller in 1957 was the 210 four-door sedan. This one is a V-8 with whitewalls and two-tone paint. It is otherwise in base form.

The more traditional buyer who wanted a dressy two-door car would be quite pleased with this 1957 Bel Air two-door sedan. While not offering as much youthful zest as the Sport Coupe, it was a solid car with a high trim level. The price was nice as well.

This 1957 Bel Air Convertible is shown with the top up and side windows down. With the exception of a V-8 engine and whitewalls, there are no options shown.

This 1957 150 six-cylinder two-door sedan is looking pretty good with whitewalls and two-tone paint. With its added bright trim, the 150 had come a long way since 1955.

A very late prototype 1957 210 two-door sedan shows the side trim treatment that was originally approved for 210 models.

'57

An assortment of 1957 accessories on display at the dealer announcement show. Note the spinner on a small hubcap to the right of the washer bottle. The Bel Air Sedan is lacking the quarter panel anodized aluminum insert, which was originally planned as an option.

Even the most hardened station wagon detractor would have to love this 1957 Nomad at least a little. Many folks will love it a lot.

Chevrolet's lowest price 1957 station wagon was this 150 Handyman six-cylinder. For a completely base vehicle, it looks unexpectedly good.

These triplets were among the early buyers of three 1957 Bel Airs. They are shown receiving the keys.

A 1957 Bel Air four-door sedan with V-8 engine and whitewalls waits at the curb in California while the owner browses an antique store for treasures to fill the generous trunk.

Car rental agencies have been good Chevrolet customers for many decades. This fleet of 1957s lined up for their class portrait. The car on the right is the only one with accessory front bumper guards.

The 210 shown here has an overdrive transmission; the overdrive handle is seen beneath the dash to the right of the steering column.

(Right) This shot of the display at the dealer announcement show reveals that the 210 side trim issue was not resolved until the last moment.

The lowest cost six-passenger 1957 Chevrolet was this six-cylinder 150 two-door sedan. It has no visible options.

A new Bel Air Convertible was rotated to a steep angle to reveal the underside (or, in this shot, the interior) to visitors at the Chevrolet dealer announcement show.

The severe belt-line dip is shown in this rear compartment shot of a 1957 Bel Air Sport Sedan.

The texture of the vinyl used in the seat inserts of the 1957 Bel Air convertible is clearly shown here. This vehicle has power windows.

The script on the front fender cove of this 1957 Corvette tells us that this car has fuel injection, a new option for 1957.

The rear
compartment
of a 1957 210
Sport Coupe
was bright and
airy. Notice
that the factory
fit on the seat
upholstery is
not up to
current judging
standards.

The beautiful waffle pattern interior of a 1957 Corvette is shown with the optional hardtop in place.

This is the beefy
undercarriage of a
1957 Chevrolet
convertible. While mud
splashed and dirty, it
still represents an
excellent reference
source for many
components.

Judges take note: The trunk bulkhead cardboard was somewhat wavy in this new 1957 Corvette.

This is what the engine compartment of a fuel-injected Corvette looked like in 1957.

The blackwalls and base hubcaps do nothing for this 1957 210 Sport Coupe but the accesssory rear-mounted antenna is a nice touch.

A 1957 Bel Air engine compartment with a 283 four-barrel, power brakes, and power steering. This made for a very nice combination of performance and convenience.

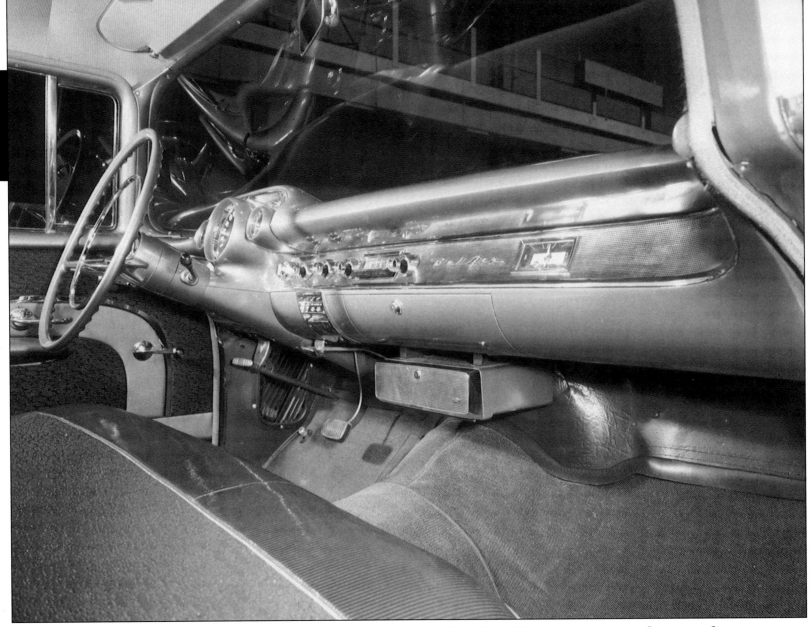

A record player has been installed in this 1957 Bel Air for evaluation. These were somewhat popular aftermarket accessories for a few years but were too primitive and costly to gain broad appeal.

The 1957 Corvette SS made its racing debut at Sebring but retired after 23 laps. The AMA ban on racing activities prevented further development work.

This angle shows off the curved rear quarter windows used on all 1957 Chevrolet station wagons. The V-8 model shown is a Bel Air Townsman six-passenger, four-door with two-tone paint and whitewalls.

This is the 1957 Corvette Super Sport one-off show car. The little blister windshields made the use of a top impossible — or at least impractical.

The Corvette SR-2 race car is seen at Daytona Beach in 1957.

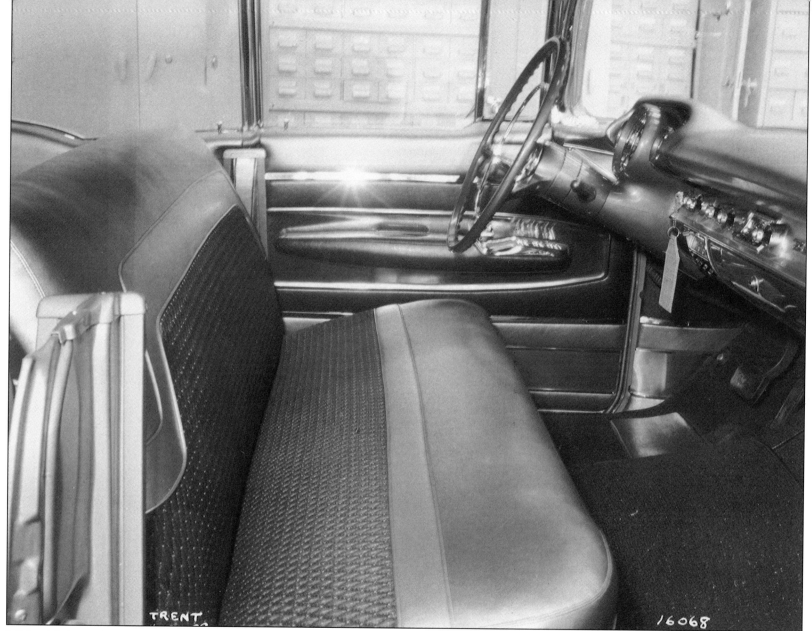

This 1957 Bel Air Sport Sedan was upgraded at Styling with an interior trim level that was close to that of an Oldsmobile 98. The door panel and kick panel treatment was closer to that which Cadillac would use in a few years.

Dated December 26, 1956, this shot was identified as "XP-64 Corvette, lighting equipment." At present we don't know if this was a rally car, a show car or something else. Whatever it was, we wouldn't want the driver to flash his lights at us.